THE BEST OF CHILDREN'S MINISTRY MAGAZINE

DEVOTIONS

110 EYE-POPPING, JAW-DROPPING CHILDREN'S MESSAGES

children's
ministry
MAGAZINE

Group

Loveland, Colorado | www.group.com

Group resources actually work!

This Group resource helps you focus on **"The 1 Thing®"**— a life-changing relationship with Jesus Christ. "The 1 Thing" incorporates our **R.E.A.L.** approach to ministry. It reinforces a growing friendship with Jesus, encourages long-term learning, and results in life transformation, because it's:

Relational
Learner-to-learner interaction enhances learning and builds Christian friendships.

Experiential
What learners experience through discussion and action sticks with them up to 9 times longer than what they simply hear or read.

Applicable
The aim of Christian education is to equip learners to be both hearers and doers of God's Word.

Learner-based
Learners understand and retain more when the learning process takes into consideration how they learn best.

THE BEST OF CHILDREN'S MINISTRY MAGAZINE DEVOTIONS
110 Eye-Popping, Jaw-Dropping Children's Messages

Copyright © 2007 Group Publishing, Inc.
Visit our Web site: **www.group.com**

All rights reserved. No part of this book may be reproduced in any manner whatsoever without prior written permission from the publisher, except where noted in the text and in the case of brief quotations embodied in critical articles and reviews. For information, e-mail Permissions at inforights@group.com or write Permissions, Group Publishing, Inc., Product Support Services Dept., P.O. Box 481, Loveland, CO 80539.

Credits

Editor: Laurie Copley
Quality Control Editor: Christine Yount Jones
Chief Creative Officer: Joani Schultz
Art Director: Josh Emrich
Print Production Artist: Greg Longbons and Julia Martin
Cover Art Director/Designer: Josh Emrich
Photography: Craig DeMartino
Production Manager: DeAnne Lear

Unless otherwise noted, Scripture taken from the HOLY BIBLE, NEW INTERNATIONAL VERSION®. Copyright © 1973, 1978, 1984 by International Bible Society. Used by permission of Zondervan Publishing House. All rights reserved.

Library of Congress Cataloging-in-Publication Data
The best of children's ministry magazine devotions. -- 1st American pbk. ed.
    p. cm.
  Includes index.
  ISBN-13: 978-0-7644-3440-2 (pbk. : alk. paper)
1. Church work with children. 2. Children--Religious life. I. Group Publishing.
BV639.C4B48 2007
268'.432--dc22

                    2006028632

10 9 8 7 6 5 4 3 2 1   16 15 14 13 12 11 10 09 08 07
Printed in the United States of America.

THANKS TO OUR TALENTED AUTHORS!

Brant Baker
Glynis Belec
Georgia Bergstrom
Katy Borgstadt
Jody Brolsma
Carolyn Caufman
Patti Chromey
Rick Chromey
Gay Correll
Andrea Couch
Susan Dietrich
Kay Eaton
Laurie Edwards
Kandi Elliott
Kim Estes
Amanda Garrett
Nanette Goings
Sheila Halasz
Kathy Jackson
Tara Jernigan
Christine Yount Jones
Vivian Jones
Janel Kauffman
Emeta Kraemer
Gary Lindsay
Susan L. Lingo
Neil MacQueen
Dalinda Marshall
Brian Mason
Joy Mason
Tim McCracken
Karen McDuff
Ken McDuff
Laura Meyers

Karela Moffat
Barbie Murphy
Lori Niles
Kevin Olson
Nancy Paulson
Melinda Reid
Bev Scott
Julie Shaffer
Dawn Smith
Mark Sprague
Sue Steele
Judy Stewart
Esther Stockwell
Genie Stoker
Susan Taulbee
Janice Thatcher
Peter Theodore Jr.
Debbie Thompson
Barbara Vogelgesang
Jim Vogelgesang
Susan Waterman Voss
Merilyn Waldron
Heather Ward
Teresa Welch
Rick White
Jennifer Root Wilger
Keith Wilson
Michelle Wolf
Chuck Yeager
Carol Younger
Malinda Zellman

CONTENTS

CONTENTS

CONTENTS

INTRODUCTION

No children's ministry program is complete without devotions as an integral component. But devotions that kids enjoy—and remember—aren't always easy to come up with.

That's why we've done the work for you! We've taken 110 of the best devotion ideas from Children's Ministry Magazine and put them all into one easy-to-use book. Gleaned from issues spanning the past 10 years, these creative devotions are more than just fun and easy to lead; they also teach kids important Bible truths they'll actually remember.

Children's ministry experts from all over the country have contributed these devotion ideas, so we know they work! The helpful indexes make it possible to search by Scripture reference or by age level, so finding the most effective devotion for your lesson will be easy.

Use this collection of best devotion ideas

• as an instant resource when you need an instant devotion,

• to plan devotions for your next special event,

• to fill in the gaps of your curriculum, and

• to offer as a resource to help volunteers in their planning of events.

Keep this book handy—you'll use it often!

THE BEST OF

children's
ministry
MAGAZINE

CHAPTER ONE

OLD TESTAMENT

CREATION STATIONS

Kids celebrate God's creation.
Text: Genesis 1:1–2:2

WHAT YOU'LL NEED:

You'll need for each child a flashlight, a balloon, a cup of dirt, and a snack.

FOR EXTRA IMPACT:

- Let kids each make a creation collage using craft supplies such as yarn, ribbon, buttons, fabric scraps, leaves, and stickers.

- Have kids form pairs and explain their collages.

- Teach kids the words to this prayer:

  Thank you, God, for the world you made.

  I will praise you every day.

ALLERGY ALERT

Be aware that some children have food allergies that can be dangerous. Know your children, and consult with parents about allergies their children may have. Also be sure to read food labels carefully as hidden ingredients can cause allergy-related problems.

DIRECTIONS

Designate seven stations. Place the following props, one for each child, at the stations: a flashlight (Station 1), a balloon (Station 2), a cup of dirt (Station 3), and a snack (Station 7). Have children leave the props at each station.

Station 1: In the beginning, God said, "Let there be light." (Turn off the lights, and turn on the flashlights.)

2: On the second day, God created the sky. (Inflate and release balloons.)

3: God made the seas and land. (Smell and touch the dirt in the cups.)

4: On the fourth day, God created the sun, moon, and stars. (Recite "Twinkle, Twinkle Little Star.")

5: God made living things, including birds. ("Fly" around the room.)

6: God made people in his own image. (Shake each other's hand, and say, "Pleased to meet you.")

7: God rested and made the day holy. (Have kids enjoy a snack while resting.)

THE IMAGE

Kids learn about respecting others.
Text: Genesis 1:27

WHAT YOU'LL NEED:

You'll need a Bible and an instant-print camera and film.

FOR EXTRA IMPACT:

- Take pictures of each child, and put the photos on a bulletin board with this heading, "We are all created in God's image."

- Ask: What does it mean to be created in God's image? How can knowing that you're created in God's image change the way you act?

- Close in prayer, asking God to help kids grow more like Jesus every day.

DIRECTIONS

Take one child aside ahead of time, and quietly explain that you'll take a picture of him or her and then destroy it.

Take a picture of the volunteer. As it develops, discuss how it's an image of the person. Admire the picture for a minute, then crush it, throw it on the ground, and step on it. Respond to the children's reactions.

Say: It's just an image. I didn't hurt the real person. Why would anyone be upset about what I did?

Read aloud **Genesis 1:27.** Say: People are created in God's image; it's like we're pictures of God.

Ask: Did I treat our friend's photo with respect and dignity? Why or why not? How do you think God feels when we don't treat people, who are made in his image, with respect? What kind of respectful words should we say to people who are created in God's image?

Say: You are created in God's image. Every day you are becoming more and more like him as you grow in Christ. Let's show respect for God by the way we treat each other.

CREATION PUZZLE

Kids learn about creation vs. evolution.
Text: Genesis 2:4-7

WHAT YOU'LL NEED:

You'll need a Bible, a puzzle, and a ticking timer.

FOR EXTRA IMPACT:

- Have kids color their own creation scenes on card stock and write, "God created the heavens and the earth."

- Have kids cut their pictures into puzzle pieces and place the pieces in envelopes. Let kids trade their puzzles with partners and put the new puzzles together.

- Challenge each child to give his or her puzzle to a friend and tell that person how God created the world.

DIRECTIONS

Dump the puzzle onto the floor. Have kids sit in a circle around the puzzle. Say: Evolution teaches that the world created itself over a very long period of time. The Bible teaches that the world and all its inhabitants were created by God in six days.

Let's see how long this puzzle takes to put itself together. Concentrate on the puzzle, and imagine the pieces jumping together.

Start the timer and say, "Go." After the kids realize nothing is going to happen, have them cheer for the puzzle to put itself together. Stop the timer when you think the kids have gotten the point.

Ask: How long do you think it would take for the puzzle to put itself together? What is needed for the puzzle to be put together? It takes someone with wisdom and power to put a puzzle together, just as it took someone with wisdom and power to create the earth.

Read aloud **Genesis 2:4-7.** Finish the lesson by having the kids put the puzzle together.

MOSES IN A BASKET

Kids learn that God protects them.
Text: Exodus 2:1-10

WHAT YOU'LL NEED:

You'll need a Bible, dinner-roll dough, Hershey's Kisses chocolates, cinnamon and sugar in a bowl, melted margarine in a bowl, a large spoon, a cookie sheet, and an oven.

ALLERGY ALERT
See page 10.

FOR EXTRA IMPACT:

- Play praise music as kids sit in a circle and pass a "Moses" doll in a basket. When you stop the music, the child holding the basket can share one way God has protected him or her.

- Ask: How does knowing that God protects you help you face new situations? Explain.

- Teach kids this rhyme:

  God protects me in every way.

  He keeps me safe both night and day.

DIRECTIONS

Read aloud **Exodus 2:1-10.** Say: God protected Moses. Give each child a Hershey's Kiss to unwrap but not eat.

Say: Pretend this candy is Moses. Moses' mother knew he was in danger. She made a watertight basket. Wrap your roll tightly around Moses. Make sure your "basket" is tightly sealed.

Moses' mother placed him in the river and asked God to protect him. Float your basket in the melted margarine. Have kids roll their dough in the margarine and remove with a spoon.

Say: God placed Pharaoh's daughter next to the river. She had the basket pulled up onto the sandy shore. Dip your basket into the cinnamon-sugar "sand."

Pharaoh's daughter took care of baby Moses in her home. Have kids place their baskets on a cookie sheet.

Bake the rolls in a 350-degree oven for about 15 minutes.

As children eat, ask: How has God protected you from harm?

CHOOSE LIFE

Kids learn that God gives us choices.
Text: Deuteronomy 30:15-19

WHAT YOU'LL NEED:

You'll need a Bible, milk chocolate squares, bitter chocolate squares, and paper bags.

ALLERGY ALERT
See page 10.

FOR EXTRA IMPACT:

- Give each pair three cups and a small ball. Have partners take turns hiding the ball under a cup, quickly moving the cups around, and then guessing where the ball is. Ask: How is deciding which cup to choose like or unlike how we decide to follow God's commands?

- Ask: How do you think God feels when we don't obey him? How does obeying God show our love for him?

- Give each child a piece of milk chocolate candy. As kids enjoy the sweet treat, have them think about God's sweet promises for those who choose to walk in his ways.

DIRECTIONS

Place one square of milk chocolate per child in one paper bag, and put two squares of bitter chocolate per child in another paper bag.

Say: I have chocolate for you today, but you have to choose which kind you want. You can take two squares from this bag or one square from this bag.

After kids choose, let them taste the chocolate. Ask: How do you feel about your choice? Explain. What other choices have you made this week, such as what to eat or which friend to hang out with? What choices have you ever made that disappointed you?

Say: Let me tell you about a very important choice we all have to make. Read aloud **Deuteronomy 30:15-19**. Ask: What is this passage talking about? Why does God command us to follow his ways? What does he promise us if we choose him? How can we walk in God's ways?

ON THE INSIDE

Kids learn about looking at the heart.
Text: 1 Samuel 16:7

WHAT YOU'LL NEED:

You'll need a Bible, wet wipes, a caramel apple for each child, and a red onion covered with caramel to look like a caramel apple.

See page 10.

FOR EXTRA IMPACT:

- Ask: Why does God look at a person's heart instead of outward appearance?

- Ask: Why should we look at others' hearts instead of judging them by their looks?

- Have kids think of a time they judged someone's outward appearance. Then close in prayer, asking God's forgiveness and his help in looking at others' hearts.

▶ DIRECTIONS

Give each child a caramel apple. Choose a child with a good sense of humor to give the onion to, or let the child in on the onion-apple secret ahead of time. Ask the child to react dramatically when discovering the onion.

Have children stand in a circle. Say: I've brought a treat for you to enjoy today. Let's eat!

Have kids bite into their snacks. Watch to see the reaction of the child who has the caramel onion. After the commotion has cleared, give that child a real caramel apple.

Ask: How was the outside of the caramel onion similar to or different from the caramel apples? How about the inside?

Read aloud **1 Samuel 16:7.** Say: Describe how people are sometimes great on the outside but not so great on the inside. How are people sometimes not very appealing on the outside but really great people on the inside? How can you discover the inside of people and not just go by their outward appearances?

SPECIAL TO GOD

Kids learn that God loves everyone.
Text: 1 Samuel 16:7

WHAT YOU'LL NEED:

You'll need a Bible and a framed mirror.

FOR EXTRA IMPACT:

- Set out markers, crayons, glue, yarn, fabric scraps, and other craft supplies. Let kids each create a self-portrait using the supplies.

- Have kids form pairs and show each other their portraits. Then have partners affirm each other by naming things that are special about each other.

- Display kids' portraits in the hall, and invite other classes and church members to a showing of these special creations.

▶ DIRECTIONS

Hold up the mirror so only you can look into it. Say: I'm looking at a picture of someone God says is very special. Would you like to see the picture? OK, but I'll show you only if you promise not to tell who's in the picture.

Hold the mirror up to each child so only one child can see into it at a time.

Ask: Did we all see the same person? Who did you see? God thinks we're all special. God thinks you're special. Which child here do you think is God's favorite child? God doesn't have a favorite, does he?

Say: The person you saw in the picture doesn't look exactly like the other children. Some of you have dark hair; others have light hair. Some have dark skin; others have light skin. Some are tall; others are short. But no matter how you look, God thinks you're special.

God says that what makes us special is what's inside, not how we look on the outside. Read aloud **1 Samuel 16:7.** Say: Let's thank God for making each of us special and unique.

Close in prayer.

WHAT'S A LEADER?

Kids learn about leadership.
Text: 1 Kings 3:9-10

WHAT YOU'LL NEED:

You'll need a Bible and a small object.

FOR EXTRA IMPACT:

- Ask: Why is it important to ask God to help us know right from wrong?

- Ask: Why do you think it pleases God when we ask for his help?

- Close in prayer, asking that God help kids turn to him for guidance.

 DIRECTIONS

Keep the object hidden from the kids. Say: Everyone close your eyes, and then I'll hold up an object. You need to guess what the object is. You may not touch the object, and there will be no hints. OK, any guesses?

Let kids guess as they keep their eyes closed. Ask: Would you like a hint?

Choose one child to look and give clues. Say: Our leader will give clues to help you guess.

When someone correctly guesses the object, have all children open their eyes. Ask: How did you feel when you couldn't guess the object? How did you feel when our leader helped you guess?

Read aloud **1 Kings 3:9-10.** Have kids tell about a time they couldn't do something on their own.

Say: Leaders help us do things we can't do on our own. Ask: What are some qualities of a leader? How can you serve God as a leader in your school or with your friends?

CORNUCOPIA OF THANKS

Kids learn about thankfulness.
Text: 1 Chronicles 16:8, 12

WHAT YOU'LL NEED:

You'll need a Bible, a cornucopia or basket, an apple, a toy car, a stuffed animal, a ring, a key, a school paper, and other items that'll help kids remember things they're thankful for.

FOR EXTRA IMPACT:

- Have kids each decorate a sheet of brown construction paper to resemble the weave of a basket. Then roll the paper into a cone shape, and tape the edges to make a cornucopia.

- On small pieces of paper, have kids write about or draw pictures of things they're thankful to God for. Have kids roll the papers like scrolls, tie them with ribbon, and place them in their cornucopias.

- Encourage kids to open one of the scrolls each day and give thanks to God for his good gifts.

DIRECTIONS

Read aloud **1 Chronicles 16:8, 12.** Say: God told the people of Israel to remember his works. That's a great thing for us to do every day.

Show the cornucopia. Say: This is a traditional basket. Just by looking at it, I'm reminded of Thanksgiving. Inside are some items that might remind you of things to thank God for. For example, when I pull out this apple, you might think of all the good food God has provided for you. Or you might thank God for good health. When I show you something from the cornucopia, get ready to tell how it reminds you of some way that God has blessed you. After each item, we'll all say "Thank you, God."

Have kids respond to the items. Ask: Are you surprised at some of the things you remembered? Why do you think it's important to remember what God has done?

CHEATER, CHEATER

Kids learn what the Bible says about cheating.
Text: Psalm 15:1-2

WHAT YOU'LL NEED:

You'll need a Bible and masking tape.

FOR EXTRA IMPACT:

- Have kids form groups of three or four. Have groups think of ways people cheat outside of school, such as when playing games or receiving too much change from a store.

- Let groups take turns leading the rest of the class in playing the agree/disagree game using the ideas groups came up with.

- Ask: Why does God want us to be honest? What's the difference in how you feel when you do right and when you do wrong? Explain.

DIRECTIONS

Make a masking-tape line on the floor. Tell kids that one end represents *agree* and the other end represents *disagree*.

Say: I'll make a statement. If you agree with it, go to the agree end. If you disagree, go to the disagree end. If you're not sure, go to the middle.

Here are the statements (pause between statements):

It's OK to look at someone else's paper when you're taking a test.

If I need help with my homework, it's OK to ask a friend for help.

It's OK to copy part of a report straight from an encyclopedia.

If you don't have time to read a book, it's OK just to rent the movie based on the book.

Read aloud **Psalm 15:1-2.**

Ask: What does this Scripture say about cheating? Even if someone doesn't get caught cheating, how do you think God feels about it? Why do kids cheat? How can we avoid cheating at school this year?

Say: Let's commit to being honest in our schoolwork.

Close in prayer.

COOKIE CONNECTION

Kids learn a tasty lesson about experiencing faith.
Text: Psalm 34:8

WHAT YOU'LL NEED:

You'll need a Bible and a package of your group's favorite cookies.

ALLERGY ALERT
See page 10.

FOR EXTRA IMPACT:

- Have kids share different ways they've experienced God's goodness. Ask: How can we share God's goodness with others?

- Ask: What does it mean to take refuge in the Lord? How does that bring blessings?

- For each child, you'll need a copy of the Scripture verse, a baggie, and another cookie. Have kids put the verse and a cookie in a baggie and then share the treat and Scripture with a friend or family member.

DIRECTIONS

Say: We're going to have cookies for a snack. First, let's find out everything there is to know about these cookies.

Read aloud the information on the package back. Then ask: Why do you like these cookies? How do you eat them? What do they smell, feel, and look like?

Give each child an opportunity to say something. Then pass out the cookies, and let the children enjoy them.

Say: Which do you think is better—eating these cookies or talking about them? Explain. Our experience with these cookies today is like faith. Ask: What did we do to experience these cookies more? How can we experience our faith more? Why isn't it enough to just talk about or know about our faith?

Read aloud **Psalm 34:8.**

TASTE AND SEE

Kids learn about knowing God.
Text: Psalm 34:8

WHAT YOU'LL NEED:

You'll need a Bible, a large screen, and enough dried pineapple for each child.

ALLERGY ALERT
See page 10.

FOR EXTRA IMPACT:

- Ask: Why do you think God gives us good things? How do you think God feels when he gives us good gifts?

- Have kids tell ways they can show God they're thankful for the good things he gives them.

- Close in prayer, letting each child thank God for a specific blessing.

DIRECTIONS

Hide the pineapple behind the screen. Ask a child to go behind the screen. Give this child some dried pineapple.

Say: Our volunteer will pretend that you've never tasted this treat. Our volunteer will describe how the treat tastes without telling us what it is. We'll guess what our volunteer is eating.

Have the hidden child describe the taste as kids guess for no more than two minutes.

Ask: How hard or easy is it to guess what the treat is just by hearing one person describe it? How can we better know what the treat is and what it tastes like?

Bring the volunteer back and give each child dried pineapple. Ask: How is listening to someone describe the treat different from eating the treat yourself?

Read aloud **Psalm 34:8.** Ask: What are ways we can "taste and see that the Lord is good"?

CLEAN ALL OVER

Kids learn about having pure hearts.
Text: Psalm 51:10

WHAT YOU'LL NEED:

You'll need a Bible, a toothbrush and toothpaste, shampoo and a comb, soap and a washcloth, a fingernail brush and clippers, and a cross or picture of a cross.

FOR EXTRA IMPACT:

- Ask: What are things we can do to keep our hearts pure?

- Give each child a cardboard cross to decorate. Then have kids each cut out a smaller construction paper heart to glue in the center of the cross.

- Encourage kids to hang their crosses in their rooms at home to remind them that only Jesus can make their hearts clean and pure.

DIRECTIONS

Set out the pairs of hygiene items, one at a time, in the order listed. Ask the following questions after you set out each pair. What's the purpose of these items? How do they work?

Show the cross, and read aloud **Psalm 51:10.** Say: There's no soap for the inside of us, but Jesus came so that we could have clean, pure hearts. Ask: Why is it important to have a clean body? Why is it important to have a clean heart?

Close in prayer, thanking God for giving us Jesus so our hearts can be cleansed.

ROCK SOLID

Kids learn about God's dependability.
Text: Psalm 71:3

WHAT YOU'LL NEED:

You'll need a Bible, cornstarch, water, a measuring cup, a fist-sized rock, a mixing bowl, and paper towels.

ALLERGY ALERT
See page 10.

FOR EXTRA IMPACT:

- Ask: Why do you think God wants to be our rock and our fortress? What does that mean in your life?

- Ask: When do you need to turn to God for refuge?

- Give each child a small rock to keep as a reminder that God is our rock and refuge.

DIRECTIONS

Dissolve 2 cups cornstarch in 1 cup of water. If the "goo" mixture won't form a ball when squeezed, add more cornstarch. The substance will immediately return to a liquid form after each time it is handled.

Gather the children in a circle, give each child a paper towel, and pass the rock around the circle. Say: As you hold this rock, say one word to describe it.

Shape a portion of the cornstarch mixture into a ball in the bowl. Pass the bowl to one of the children and watch what happens. Say: When you're given this bowl, shape the goo into a ball. Then place the ball back in the bowl and pass it on. Use the paper towels to wipe your hands.

Say: One of the words we often use to describe rocks is *solid*. Is this ball of goo solid? It really isn't very dependable. Listen to what the Bible says about God.

Read aloud **Psalm 71:3.** Say: God is often called a rock. Ask: Since rocks are solid, what are some things they can be used for? Could the goo be used for those things? Why or why not? If God is like a rock and everything else is like the goo, what happens when we depend on God? when we depend on other things besides God?

Close in prayer, thanking God for being so dependable.

FEAR NOT

Kids learn that God is our protector.
Text: Psalm 91

WHAT YOU'LL NEED:

You'll need a Bible and scrap paper.

FOR EXTRA IMPACT:

- Play the game again, and let each child have a turn to be "It." Ask: Which role did you like best, being inside the shelter, being the shelter, or throwing the wads? Why?

- Ask: How can knowing that God is your shelter help you the next time you're afraid?

- Have kids each take a paper wad, open it, and press the paper flat. Have kids write, "The Lord is my refuge and fortress...I trust in him" on their papers.

DIRECTIONS

Distribute scrap paper, and have kids wad the paper as you talk. Ask: When are times you're afraid? The Bible tells us that we have nothing to fear with God on our side.

Read aloud **Psalm 91:1-10.** Say: Let's act out these verses.

Choose a child to be "It." Have half the children use their bodies to make a shelter to protect "It." Have the other half try to hit "It" with the paper wads. After two minutes of play, stop the action.

Ask: How did you feel in the shelter? How easy or difficult was your job of protecting "It"? How did your shelter compare with the way **Psalm 91** describes God's shelter?

Say: You are God's precious treasure. He is greater than any evil on this earth. God will protect you. Listen to what God says about you.

Read aloud **Psalm 91:14-16,** personalizing the Scripture by using the pronoun *you*.

Close in prayer, thanking God for his love and protection.

EGGSTRA PROTECTION

Kids learn about God's protection.
Text: Psalm 91:1-2

WHAT YOU'LL NEED:

You'll need a Bible, an empty pint-sized milk carton, cotton balls, a raw egg, strapping tape, and a bowl.

FOR EXTRA IMPACT:

- Ask: How is the protection the milk carton provides for the egg like or unlike the protection God provides for us?

- Ask: What do you think it means to rest in God's shadow?

- Ask: How can knowing that God is your protector change your life?

DIRECTIONS

Before kids arrive, fill one-third of the milk carton with cotton balls. Carefully place the egg in the center of the carton, and then completely fill the carton with cotton balls. Tape the opening shut.

Have kids sit in a circle. Say: I put an egg in this milk carton. What do you think will happen if we toss it to each other?

Toss the milk carton to a child, and have that child toss the carton to another child. Continue until each child has tossed it.

Say: Let's see what happened to the egg.

Open the milk carton and remove the egg, being careful not to show the cotton balls. Crack the egg into the bowl. Ask: Why do you think the egg didn't break?

Show kids the cotton balls. Ask: How did the cotton balls protect the egg?

Read aloud **Psalm 91:1-2.** Ask: What do these verses say about God? How does God protect us and keep us safe?

Close in prayer, thanking God for his protection.

EVERY COLOR UNDER HEAVEN

Kids learn about taking care of creation.
Text: Psalm 104:24

WHAT YOU'LL NEED:

You'll need a Bible and a container of M&M'S or Skittles candies.

ALLERGY ALERT
See page 10.

FOR EXTRA IMPACT:

- Read aloud **Psalm 104:24.** Ask: Why does God want us to care for his creation?

- Have kids list specific things they can do to take care of God's creation, such as picking up litter on the church grounds or at their schools.

- Let kids choose one thing they'd like to do as a group to care for God's creation, then plan a special time when kids can work together to do the selected task.

DIRECTIONS

Form three groups. Say the phrases, and give groups the assignments.

Group 1—"Oh, Lord, how many are your works." With your group, choose a number between one and five.

Group 2—"In wisdom, you made them all." Shake out the number of candies that Group 1 chooses.

Group 3—"The earth is full of your possessions." Your group has 15 seconds to call out things in God's creation, using the number chosen and the color of candies.

Say: For example, if Group 1 calls out "two" and Group 2 shakes out red and yellow, Group 3 has to name two red things in God's creation, such as a flower and ladybug, and two yellow things, such as the sun and a lemon.

After each round, rotate the groups' responsibilities. After three rounds, share the candy with everyone.

Ask: How do things in creation meet people's needs? Do you think people are taking good care of God's creation? Why or why not? If God put you in charge of his creation, what would you do?

Say: God has put each of us in charge of his creation. God wants us to take care of what he has created.

EXTREME BLESSINGS

Kids learn that obedience brings blessings.
Text: Psalm 119:34-35

WHAT YOU'LL NEED:

You'll need a Bible.

FOR EXTRA IMPACT:

- Ask: Why is it important to obey God? Explain.

- Ask: Why do you think obeying God makes us happy?

- Close in prayer, asking God to help kids be obedient to him.

▶ DIRECTIONS

Have children stand. Form two groups. Assign one group to be the "sad group" and the other group to be the "happy group."

Say: When you hear your group name, show your emotion. Let's practice. Sad group, show your emotion. Now, happy group, show your emotion.

Everybody wants to be extremely blessed by God and happy. No one enjoys being sad. People will try anything to be happy. When they're sad, they may change friends, play sports, or watch funny shows. While trying to be happy, they sometimes even disobey God by stealing things, being selfish, or lying. But doing these things only makes them sad.

The Bible tells us in this psalm that extreme obedience to God brings extreme blessing or happiness to our lives.

Read aloud **Psalm 119:35.** Say: The writer of Psalm 119 wrote about wanting to do the right thing.

Read aloud **Psalm 119:34.** Ask: Why do you think this person wanted to obey God? Doing what God says to do makes us happy. Let's all show by our faces that we want to choose obedience and happiness. Now we're happy!

THE DIARY

Kids learn about God's knowledge and care.
Text: Psalm 139:16

WHAT YOU'LL NEED:

You'll need a Bible and paper and pencil for each child.

FOR EXTRA IMPACT:

- Have kids each make a diary by folding several sheets of paper in half and stapling the fold. Let kids each decorate the front cover and write the words to **Psalm 139:16** on an inside page.

- Encourage kids to take their diaries home and write in them each day to record the wonderful things God has done in their lives.

- Later, let kids bring their diaries in and share praise reports with the rest of the class.

▶ DIRECTIONS

Form pairs. Give each child a sheet of paper and a pencil. Say: This is your diary. A diary is a book people write in to remember things that happened to them. Fold your paper in half. Write your name on your diary, then give it to your partner.

Say: This is a future diary. Write in your partner's diary what'll happen to him or her this week—things your partner will do, think, and say.

Pause for one minute. Then ask: You can't do that? Why not? OK, take your diary, and write about the coming week for yourself.

Pause for one minute. Then ask: You can't do that either?

Read aloud **Psalm 139:16.** Say: None of us can write what we or our friends will do until we've done it! But what does this passage say God has done? How can he do that? How does this verse make you feel about God?

Close with a prayer of thanks for how God knows and cares for us.

WORDS THAT KILL

Kids learn about put-downs and hurtful words.
Text: Proverbs 15:1

WHAT YOU'LL NEED:

You'll need a Bible, paper, pencils, and a paper bag.

FOR EXTRA IMPACT:

- Have kids race to throw the paper wads in a trash can. Afterward, ask: How was throwing the wads in the trash can like or unlike what God would want us to do with harsh words? Explain.

- Have kids list kind words they can say to others.

- Give each child a small flat stone with "Proverbs 15:1" written on it. Encourage kids to keep their stones as reminders to use kind words.

DIRECTIONS

Say: When I was young, children used to say, "Sticks and stones may break my bones, but words can never hurt me." Do you think that's true? Why or why not?

Have children each write a put-down on a sheet of paper and wad it up. Place all the put-downs in a paper bag. One by one, read each put-down and throw it at the children. Then read aloud **Proverbs 15:1.**

Ask: How did it feel to be pelted with put-downs? Why do kids say mean things to each other? What does this verse in Proverbs say harsh words do? What about gentle words?

Say: This week, let's remember to say kind things to people rather than harsh words.

Close in prayer.

FRIENDS FOREVER

Kids learn about friendship.
Text: Proverbs 18:24

WHAT YOU'LL NEED:

You'll need a Bible and a puppet.

FOR EXTRA IMPACT:

- Ask: What can we do to be a good friend to others? How is Jesus a good friend to us?

- Help kids list things they can do to show their friends that they love them.

- Challenge kids to choose one thing from the list to do for one of their friends during the week.

DIRECTIONS

The Script:

Puppet: *(Sighs.)*

Leader: Something seems to be wrong with [puppet's name]. [Puppet's name], what's wrong?

Puppet: My heart hurts.

Leader: Should I take you to the doctor?

Puppet: I don't need a heart doctor. It's not that kind of hurt…it's just that…

Leader: You're sad…

Puppet: Yeah…*(Cries.)* My best friend moved away.

Leader: Oh, now I understand. *(To children)* Have you had a friend who moved? Or have you ever moved away from your friends? It's sad, isn't it?

Puppet: I did everything with him. We rode bicycles. We climbed trees. I miss him.

Leader: [Puppet's name], you have a best friend that'll never, ever leave you.

Puppet: Who's that?

Leader: Jesus. He understands how you feel. And he loves you very, very much.

Leader: *(Reads aloud Proverbs 18:24.)*

Close in prayer, thanking God for friends.

THREE STRANDS

Kids learn about the unity of believers.
Text: Ecclesiastes 4:9-12

WHAT YOU'LL NEED:

You'll need a Bible and red shoestring licorice.

ALLERGY ALERT
See page 10.

FOR EXTRA IMPACT:

- As kids eat their licorice, have them tell ways they can show love to others.

- Ask: How do you think God feels when we work together and show love to one another? Explain.

- Close in prayer, thanking God for giving us friends to help us.

DIRECTIONS

Have children stand in pairs, and give each pair a 3-foot piece of licorice. Say: I'd like each of you to hold one end of the licorice and then pull as hard as you can on the licorice to test how strong it is.

Ask for a helper, and have the child hold three strings together at the end as you braid the three strings. Ask: What do you think will happen if we pull on this braided strand?

Choose another helper to hold your end of the braid. Have both kids pull as hard as they can. Ask: Why was this braided strand harder to break?

Read aloud **Ecclesiastes 4:9-12.** Say: Just as the licorice was stronger with three pieces together, we're stronger when we stick together. Tell a partner about a time you worked with another person to do great things.

We show other people God's love by how we love each other and work together. Take a string of licorice to remind you how strong we are when we stick together.

RIGHT OR LEFT?

Kids learn about hearing God's voice.
Text: Isaiah 30:21

WHAT YOU'LL NEED:

You'll need a Bible and blindfolds for half the children.

FOR EXTRA IMPACT:

- Ask: Why is it important to listen to God?

- Ask: What happens when we don't listen to God and instead try to go our own way?

- Pray with kids, asking God to help kids listen for his voice so they can follow and obey him.

DIRECTIONS

Say: Let's experience how God's voice helps us make good choices. Find a partner, and choose who'll wear the blindfold first. If you aren't wearing a blindfold, your job is to stay behind your partner as you guide him or her around the room with your voice. No touching! We'll do this for two minutes, and then we'll switch roles and repeat the activity.

Allow time. Then gather kids in a circle. Ask: How did you feel when you were blindfolded and relying on someone to help you move around the room?

Read aloud **Isaiah 30:21.** Ask: How was our activity like or unlike listening to God? How do we listen to God? How does listening to God help us decide what's right or wrong in our lives? How can we better listen for God's voice telling us, "This is the way—walk in it"?

THE POTTER AND THE CLAY

Kids learn that God molds us.
Text: Isaiah 64:8

WHAT YOU'LL NEED:

You'll need a Bible, clay, a pencil, a piece of poster board, and a marker.

FOR EXTRA IMPACT:

- Let children show their clay creations to the class. Say: Just as our clay creations are special, God created each one of us with special gifts.

- Have kids each tell one special thing about themselves. Close in prayer to thank God for creating everyone with unique gifts and talents.

- Hang the poster with **Isaiah 64:8** written on it on a bulletin board. Take photos of the kids with their clay creations, and put the pictures on the board for a special display.

▶ DIRECTIONS

Have two children each form a pot from a ball of clay. Assign the following words to four different volunteers: *cheating, lying, arguing,* and *complaining.* Have your volunteers come forward, say their word, and poke only one of the pots. Ask: Which pot looks better? Which pot is shaped the way it was meant to be? Explain.

Say: The Bible says God is the potter and we are the clay. Hold up a poster with **Isaiah 64:8** written on it. Read the verse aloud, and have the class repeat it after you. Then ask: What does this verse mean?

Hold up the poked pot and say: If we allow others to mold us instead of letting God mold us, we may end up looking like this pot. We won't become who God wants us to be. The Bible warns us to stay away from doing wrong things. Friends sometimes want you to do wrong things such as disobeying your parents or cheating. You can learn to say no, so you can do what's right.

Give children each a piece of clay, and let them form their own creation. Remind them as they're working that, as the creator, they can make the clay into something they like, just as God makes us into something he likes.

HIDE 'N' SEEK

Kids learn about seeking God.
Text: Jeremiah 29:12-13

WHAT YOU'LL NEED:

You'll need a Bible; a large sheet of paper; a pen; red, green, and black jelly beans; and a magnifying glass.

ALLERGY ALERT
See page 10.

FOR EXTRA IMPACT:

- Ask: Why does God want us to pray to him? Why does God want us to seek him with all our hearts?

- Give kids each a piece of wax paper with an outline of a small heart drawn on it. Let kids place jelly beans on the outline to make a heart.

- Have kids find a partner and take turns telling ways they can seek God. Kids can eat one jelly bean after sharing each idea. Continue until kids eat all of their jelly beans.

DIRECTIONS

Beforehand, write **Jeremiah 29:12-13** in large letters on a sheet of paper. Hide the paper and some green, red, and black jelly beans in your room.

Walk in with a magnifying glass and start searching high and low. After a while, find what you've been looking for—the Bible verse for today. Make a big deal of showing it to the children, and then, with the magnifying glass, read it to the kids.

Say: We're going to learn more about seeking today. We're going to play Hide 'n' Seek. One-third of you will look for green jelly beans, one-third of you will look for red jelly beans, and the other third will look for black jelly beans.

Allow time for kids to search for the jelly beans. Tell them how many jelly beans you've hidden.

Ask: How did you know what to look for? What kinds of treasures do you think God may have hidden for you? How can you hunt for God's treasures?

Read aloud **Jeremiah 29:12-13.** Say: This Bible is like a magnifying glass to help us find God. Reading the Bible helps us find out things about God. It helps us understand what God wants us to do.

Say: Let's pray. God, help us to seek you. In Jesus' name, amen.

THE BEST OF
children's ministry
M A G A Z I N E

CHAPTER TWO

NEW TESTAMENT

CANDY CANE STORY

Kids learn about the Christmas story.
Text: Matthew 1:20-21

WHAT YOU'LL NEED:

You'll need 2 red-and-white candy canes for each child. Get J-shaped candy canes with 1 large red stripe and 3 smaller red stripes.

ALLERGY ALERT
See page 10.

FOR EXTRA IMPACT:

- Read aloud **Matthew 1:20-21.** Ask: How did Jesus save us from our sins?

- Ask: Why do you think Jesus was willing to die for you?

- Lead kids in thanking God for the gift of his Son.

DIRECTIONS

Say: A long time ago, a candy maker in Indiana made the Christmas candy cane to tell the real Christmas story. He chose pure white candy for the virgin birth and to remind us that Jesus is sinless. He made the candy hard so it would remind us that Jesus is the solid rock and that all God's promises are solid.

Say: The candy maker made the candy in the shape of a J to remind us of Jesus who came to earth as a baby and became our Savior. Then the candy maker added stripes. Real candy canes have three small stripes for the blood Jesus shed for us before he went to the cross and a big stripe for the blood Jesus shed on the cross so we could have eternal life.

Give kids two candy canes. Say: Jesus came at Christmas to make a way for us to go to heaven to be with him forever. Keep one candy cane, and give the other one to someone who isn't here. Tell that person the story of the candy cane.

MY BELOVED SON

Kids learn about pleasing God.
Text: Matthew 3:13-17

WHAT YOU'LL NEED:

You'll need a Bible, a white crayon, a white sheet of paper, watercolor paints, a paintbrush, and a small glass of water.

FOR EXTRA IMPACT:

- Ask: What are things we can do to please God?

- Let kids each use a white crayons to draw a dove on a sheet of blue construction paper. Have kids take their pictures home as reminders of the Bible story.

- Challenge kids to obey God and to seek to please him in everything they do.

DIRECTIONS

Before kids arrive, use a white crayon to outline a dove on a sheet of white construction paper.

Show children the white paper with the white dove hidden on it. Don't point out the dove to them. Say: This paper reminds me of a time that something very special happened to Jesus.

Have an older child read aloud **Matthew 3:13-17** while you paint the picture from the left side of the page to the right. Show children the picture with the dove revealed.

Say: The Holy Spirit rested on Jesus in the form of a dove. What would you have thought if you had seen the dove and heard God's words? Why do you think God said he was pleased with Jesus?

Say: Let's pray. God, thank you for sending Jesus to be our example. Thank you that when we're your children you are pleased with us. Help us to be more like Jesus. In Jesus' name, amen.

LETTING YOUR LIGHT SHINE

Kids learn about good deeds.
Text: Matthew 5:14-16

WHAT YOU'LL NEED:

You'll need a Bible, a votive candle, matches, and a tin can.

FOR EXTRA IMPACT:

- Have kids cut out construction-paper candles and tape on tissue-paper flames. Have kids write **"Matthew 5:14"** on the candles as a reminder that they are to be the light of the world.

- Have kids think of one good deed to do during the coming week. Let kids each write the idea on the back of their candle and take it home as a reminder of their commitment.

- Next week, ask kids how they followed through on their ideas.

DIRECTIONS

Light the candle. Ask: What will happen if I cover the candle with this tin can? We'll leave it covered and check on it later.

Have a child read aloud **Matthew 5:14-16.** Ask: What do these verses mean? What is the light that Jesus is talking about? What can you do to let your light shine? If we didn't do the good things we talked about, what would happen to our light?

Say: Let's check on the light we hid.

Have a child lift the can. Ask: What happened to the light? Why? What can make our light go out?

Relight the candle. Ask: Where can we put our light so everyone can see it?

Have another child read aloud **Matthew 5:14-16.** Close with prayer, thanking God for the many ways the kids' light can shine for Jesus.

NEW TESTAMENT

FIRST THINGS FIRST

Kids learn about setting priorities.
Text: Matthew 6:33

WHAT YOU'LL NEED:

You'll need a Bible, a quart-size jar full of large marshmallows, and a bowl. You'll also need one pint of M&M'S candies and a cup of sugar.

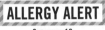
ALLERGY ALERT
See page 10.

FOR EXTRA IMPACT:

- Have kids form groups of four, and give each group marshmallows. Let kids pick one marshmallow for each way they can tell how to make God a priority in their lives.

- Have groups pray together, asking God to help them keep their priorities in order.

DIRECTIONS

Empty the jar of large marshmallows into a bowl. Say: Let's pretend that this empty jar represents our lives. The marshmallows represent God. The M&M'S are important things, such as family and friends. The sugar is the activities we do, such as school, soccer, and music lessons.

Ask: Do you think all this will fit into one jar? Let's start with the things you have to do.

Have kids name their responsibilities as you pour in the sugar, M&M'S, and then marshmallows in that order. Ask: What's wrong with our jar? Why can't everything fit in?

Remove the ingredients, and then pour in the marshmallows, M&M'S, and sugar in that order.

Read aloud **Matthew 6:33.** Ask: What happens in our lives when we don't put God first? How does putting God first help all the other areas of our lives?

TOTAL ACCEPTANCE

Kids learn about God's love.
Text: Matthew 9:9-13

WHAT YOU'LL NEED:

You'll need a Bible, a big bowl of M&M'S candies, and a small cup with 10 M&M'S candies for each child.

ALLERGY ALERT
See page 10.

FOR EXTRA IMPACT:

- Ask: Why does Jesus want us to follow him? What happens in our lives when we follow him?

- Have kids find partners. Let partners take turns telling each other ways they can follow Jesus.

- Have pairs share their ideas with the class. Challenge kids to each select one way they can follow Jesus during the week.

▶ DIRECTIONS

Say: Before Matthew followed Jesus, he was a tax collector. People didn't like him much because he was dishonest and didn't obey God's laws. He cheated.

Say: Let's pretend I'm Matthew and you're the people I collect taxes from. Your M&M'S are your "money." Look at how much money I have; I love money! By order of the Roman Empire, you must pay your taxes now. Give me three M&M'S.

Collect three candies from each child. Eat a few M&M'S. Say: Now, everyone wearing shoes, give me five more.

Collect five candies from each child, and eat more M&M'S.

Read aloud **Matthew 9:9-13.** Would you have liked Matthew? Did Jesus know what Matthew was like? Why did Jesus ask Matthew to follow him? How do you think Matthew changed after he followed Jesus? What did Jesus mean by saying, "It is not the healthy who need a doctor, but the sick"?

Say: Think of the worst thing you've ever done. Don't say it aloud.

Fill each child's cup half full of M&M'S. Say: I don't know what you're thinking, but Jesus does. No matter what you've done, Jesus will forgive you. Jesus accepts you and wants you to follow him.

Let's pray. Lord, thank you for loving and accepting us. Help us to follow you. In Jesus' name, amen.

MIRACLES HAPPEN

Kids learn about faith.
Text: Matthew 17:14-20

WHAT YOU'LL NEED:

You'll need a Bible, water, a large jar, an egg, salt, and a spoon.

ALLERGY ALERT
See page 10.

FOR EXTRA IMPACT:

- Bring in mustard seeds for kids to see. These are available in the spice section of your grocery store.

- Give each child a mustard seed, and ask: Why do you think Jesus says if we have faith as small as this mustard seed nothing is impossible?

- Have kids each tape a mustard seed to a piece of card stock. Write, "Nothing is impossible with God" on the cards.

DIRECTIONS

Hide the salt from children. Fill the jar with water, and place the egg in it.

Say: I can make this egg float in the water. Who believes me?

Have children who believe you stand on your right and children who don't believe you stand on your left. Ask: Why do you believe me? Why don't you believe me?

Read aloud **Matthew 17:14-20.** Ask: How is faith an important part of Jesus' miracles?

Have each child add salt to the water. Stir gently until the egg floats. Say: It seemed impossible that we could make the egg float. But we changed the laws at work in the water when we added the salt. The salt made the water heavier so the egg would float.

God can do the impossible because he is the ruler of the universe. God can change the rules of the universe so miracles happen. Let's praise God!

Close in prayer.

HIS SHEEP AM I

Kids learn that Jesus is our shepherd.
Text: Matthew 18:11-14

NEW TESTAMENT

WHAT YOU'LL NEED:

You'll need a Bible and a scarf. You'll also need 20 small items, such as a paper clip, a stick of gum, a pencil, and an eraser.

FOR EXTRA IMPACT:

- Ask: Have you ever lost a pet? What was that like? How is that like or unlike the way Jesus might feel if one of us were lost in sin?

- Ask: Why do you think the shepherd leaves the ninety-nine sheep to look for the lost one? What does that say about Jesus' love for us?

- Close in prayer, thanking Jesus for loving us so much that he would never leave us.

DIRECTIONS

Say: Jesus is our shepherd, and we're his sheep. What are some things a shepherd does? A shepherd is always alert and watching out for the sheep. If the sheep wander off from the flock and get into danger, the shepherd rescues them.

Set out the 20 small items, and have the children study them. Cover the items with a scarf. Have the children turn their backs for 20 seconds as you remove one or two items. Have kids turn around and tell you which items are missing.

Read aloud **Matthew 18:11-14.** Say: We're called sheep in God's Word because we need a shepherd, just as sheep do. We wander off on our own, believing that we don't need the help of our shepherd, Jesus. When we find ourselves in danger, we need Jesus' protection and guidance. Even though there are many people on this earth, Jesus knows each of us and personally watches over us. If even one person is lost or wanders away from Jesus, Jesus goes after that person to bring him or her back to him.

FORGIVE AND FORGET

Kids learn about forgiveness.
Text: Matthew 18:21-22

WHAT YOU'LL NEED:

You'll need a Bible and an unopened soft-drink can.

FOR EXTRA IMPACT:

- Form pairs, and have pairs read **Matthew 18:21-22** aloud.

- Ask: What's your reaction to the number of times Jesus tells us to forgive someone who sins against us? Do you think you could do it? Explain.

- Ask: What happens in our hearts when we forgive someone who has hurt us?

DIRECTIONS

Take children outside, and have them stand in a circle. Say: I'm going to say something I haven't yet forgiven someone for, then I'm going to throw this soft-drink can to someone else. When you catch the can, say something you need to forgive someone for, then throw it to someone else who does the same thing. We'll continue until everyone has had a chance to throw the can.

Once everyone has had a turn, have the last person with the can aim it away from the other children and open it.

Ask: What happened to the insides of the soft-drink can? What happens to our insides when we don't forgive others? When we don't forgive people and we hold our unforgiveness inside, one day we'll finally blow up. Why do you think the junk building up inside of us finally spews out?

Read aloud **Matthew 18:21-22.** Ask: How many times does Jesus say we need to forgive others? How would you feel if someone made you mad that many times in one day? What would you do? Why do you think it's so important to God that we forgive others?

Say: Let's pray silently and ask God to show us if there's anyone we need to forgive. Then let's forgive now!

Close in prayer.

DOING THE IMPOSSIBLE

Kids get creative with this near-impossible activity.
Text: Matthew 19:26

WHAT YOU'LL NEED:

You'll need a Bible and a bag of Hershey's Kisses chocolates for each group.

ALLERGY ALERT
See page 10.

FOR EXTRA IMPACT:

- Have kids pray together for those "impossible" things they're facing. Let kids report back the following week with any praise reports.

- Let kids eat some of the chocolate kisses. As they're enjoying the treat, have kids tell stories of seemingly impossible things in their lives that God made possible.

- Have kids each glue Hershey's Kisses in rows on card stock to form a cross. Then write, "'With God ALL things are possible!' (Matthew 19:26)."

DIRECTIONS

Form groups of four. Give each group a bag of Hershey's Kisses. Say: Your group can eat as many chocolate kisses as you want—as long as you don't use your hands to unwrap them.

Allow time. While this is a near-impossible task, applaud your kids' creativity and efforts.

Afterward, ask: Would you say this was an impossible task? Why or why not?

Read aloud **Matthew 19:26**. Ask: What are things that are impossible for us to do that God can do? Is there anything that is impossible for God to do? Why or why not? What's something you're facing that seems impossible? What do you think Jesus would have you do about that "impossible" thing?

UNEQUALED LOVE

Kids learn about God's love.
Text: Matthew 20:1-16

WHAT YOU'LL NEED:

You'll need a Bible and doughnuts.

ALLERGY ALERT
See page 10.

FOR EXTRA IMPACT:

- Ask: Why do you think those who worked all day were upset to receive the same pay as the workers who only worked one hour? Do you think that was fair? Explain.

- Ask: How can knowing that God loves us equally change your feelings toward others?

- Ask: What do you think the Scripture means when it says, "The last will be first, and the first will be last"?

DIRECTIONS

Say: We're going to have a race today, and the winners will get one of these doughnuts.

Have children race around the room. Then give every child a doughnut. Listen to children's remarks as you give the doughnuts.

Ask: How did you feel when you got your doughnut? How did you feel when everyone got a doughnut?

Read aloud **Matthew 20:1-16.** Ask: How was everyone getting a doughnut like or unlike this parable? Why do you think Jesus said it was good for everyone to get the same thing even though they didn't do the same work?

Say: God loves all of us equally. It doesn't matter if we're a pastor, a missionary, or a little child. God shows the same love to all of us. We can't even work more so God will love us more than someone else. God loves us the same.

Say: Let's pray. God, thank you for loving us equally. In Jesus' name, amen.

EMPTY

Kids learn about Jesus' resurrection.
Text: Matthew 28:5-7

WHAT YOU'LL NEED:

You'll need a Bible, a large towel, a hand towel, an orange, a pin, and a hollow egg.

ALLERGY ALERT
See page 10.

FOR EXTRA IMPACT:

- Ask: How would your life be different if Jesus hadn't risen from the dead? Explain.

- Give kids M&M'S candies. As kids eat the treat, have them tell new ways they can celebrate Easter.

- Close in prayer, thanking God for the sweet gift of his Son, Jesus.

DIRECTIONS

Before kids arrive, poke a small hole in each end of a room-temperature egg and blow out the contents.

Lay the towel on the floor. Say: Our lesson might be messy today.

Choose a helper, and give him or her the orange. Say: Today we're talking about trust. Do you trust gravity? If I have my helper let go of this orange, will it fall?

Have the child drop the orange. Say: Yes, gravity works; we can trust it.

Ask: What other things do you trust?

Say: Oh, I have one. What about eggs? Are they messy when you break them? Helper, hold out your hands.

Dramatically hold the egg over your helper's hands and crush it. Say: Oh! There's nothing in it!

Read aloud **Matthew 28:5-7.** Say: The third day after Jesus died, the women went to the tomb to finish preparing his body for burial. They trusted that Jesus' body would be in the tomb, but the women found the tomb as empty as this egg. Jesus had risen—just as he had promised.

PUZZLED

Kids learn that God helps us solve our problems.
Text: Luke 1:37

WHAT YOU'LL NEED:

You'll need a Bible, 3 same-color sheets of poster board, a marker, and scissors.

FOR EXTRA IMPACT:

- Give kids small pieces of poster board or card stock to make individual puzzles. Have them write the words of **Luke 1:37** on their papers, cut the papers into puzzle shapes, and then place the pieces in an envelope.

- Encourage kids to give their puzzles to a friend or family member as they explain that God helps us solve our problems.

- Let kids each make another puzzle to take home and keep as a reminder that nothing is impossible with God.

DIRECTIONS

Write the words of **Luke 1:37** in large letters on each sheet of poster board. Cut each poster board into puzzle shapes. Write "1" on the back of each piece of the first puzzle, "2" on the back of the second puzzle's pieces, and "3" on the back of the third puzzle's pieces. Mix all the pieces, and put them in one pile.

Have kids work together to put the puzzle together.

Say: You don't have all the information you need. Here's a clue.

Gather all the puzzle pieces. Form three teams. Say: I've written a number on the back of each piece. All the 1s make one puzzle; all the 2s make another, and all the 3s make a third.

Assign each team a number, and have kids put their team's puzzle together.

Ask: What was it like when you first tried to put the puzzle together? How did you feel after I gave you the clue? What is a puzzle or problem in your life right now? How can God help?

Say: God knows we have problems that seem impossible, but nothing is impossible for him. We can ask God to help us solve our problems.

LIGHT OF THE WORLD

Kids celebrate the birth of Jesus.
Text: Luke 2:1-20

WHAT YOU'LL NEED:

You'll need a Bible. For each child, you'll need a small flashlight or a construction-paper candle with a tissue-paper flame.

ALLERGY ALERT
See page 10.

FOR EXTRA IMPACT:

- Let kids use a plastic knife to cut a candle-flame shape from a slice of American cheese. Have kids carefully press the cheese flame around a pretzel rod to make a candlestick snack.

- Let kids make construction-paper candles with tissue-paper flames to give to a friend. Encourage kids to tell the friends that Jesus is the light of the world.

- Lead kids in a prayer thanking God for sending Jesus to be our light. Ask God to help kids each be a light to others.

DIRECTIONS

Ask: Who's afraid of the dark sometimes? What makes you feel afraid when it's dark? If someone turns on a light when you're feeling afraid in the darkness, how do you feel?

Have the children cover their eyes while they stand and try to touch the shoulder of someone near them. Say: You may open your eyes now and touch your friend's shoulder.

Have children sit down. Ask: Was it easier to find your friend in the dark or in the light? Why do we need light?

Say: I have a story to tell you about some people who were looking for a very important kind of light. This story is in the Bible, and it tells about the birth of a very special baby who was born to be the light of the world.

Paraphrase **Luke 2:1-20.** Say: I have a little light for each of you to take with you so you can remember to let Jesus' light shine through you. After I give you a light, turn it on, and we'll sing "This Little Light of Mine."

After singing one verse, send the children back to their seats carrying their lights while singing the song.

SANTA

Kids learn about the real meaning of Christmas.
Text: Luke 2:1-20

WHAT YOU'LL NEED:

You'll need a Bible and a sack filled with small unbreakable Christmas decorations, including Santas, elves, wreaths, stars, Nativity scenes, Rudolph, shepherds, wise men, stables, and presents. Have mangers and several figures of baby Jesus, Mary, and Joseph.

FOR EXTRA IMPACT:

- Have costumes and props on hand, and let kids act out the Christmas story.

- Let kids make their own Nativity set. Glue a large wooden bead onto each of two small clay pots turned upside down. Place fabric strips over one of the pots for Mary's "head" and over the "shoulder" of the other pot for Joseph. Place straw and a bead to represent baby Jesus inside a third pot.

- For an added touch, help kids draw faces on their Nativity figures using fine-tipped permanent markers.

DIRECTIONS

Have children take turns taking decorations from the sack. Then have them put the decorations in two separate piles—one pile representing the real meaning of Christmas and the other pile representing things that aren't the real meaning of Christmas.

Say: Let's put away the Santas, reindeer, elves, and all those things that are fun but aren't really what Christmas is all about. Now I'd like you to tell me the real story of Christmas using these decorations.

After kids tell the story, read aloud **Luke 2:1-20.** Then close in prayer, thanking God for sending the greatest gift of all—his Son, Jesus.

NEW TESTAMENT

BIBLE FRIENDS

This devotion helps nurture your kids' friendship with Jesus.
Text: Luke 5:17-26

WHAT YOU'LL NEED:

You'll need a Bible and a beach towel.

ALLERGY ALERT
See page 10.

FOR EXTRA IMPACT:

- Have teams race to cross a finish line carrying a doll or stuffed animal on a beach towel. Then have kids discuss whether it was easier lifting their teammates on the towel or racing with the dolls to the finish line. Ask: How can Jesus help us when we have to do hard things?

- Have kids each spread a graham cracker "mat" with frosting, then add a stick figure made from Twizzler's candy pieces. Add a miniature marshmallow for the head.

- As kids eat their snacks, ask: What are things we can do to help our friends when they're sick? When they're sad? When they're lonely?

▶ DIRECTIONS

Form groups of six. Lay a beach towel on the floor. Have groups take turns doing the following: Have one of the children in the group lie on the towel. Have the other group members try to pick up that child. Don't allow children to lift the child more than 6 inches off the floor. Allow each group to take its turn.

Ask: Was it hard to lift the children off the floor? Why or why not? What would you think if I asked you to carry this person downtown to the doctor?

Say: The Bible tells of some friends who carried their sick friend to Jesus. Let's read about it.

Read aloud **Luke 5:17-26.** Then ask: How did this man's friends show they loved him? How did Jesus show this man that he loved him?

Say: Jesus was a friend to this man because he helped him get well. How has Jesus been a friend to you? How has he helped you?

IT'S A GOOD THING

WHAT YOU'LL NEED:

You'll need 2 boxes, wrapping paper, tape, and small gifts for the children, such as candy canes or bookmarks.

ALLERGY ALERT
See page 10.

FOR EXTRA IMPACT:

- Ask: Why do you think God wants to give us good gifts?

- Ask: What's the best gift God ever gave you or your family? Why was it so special?

- Have kids wrap a piece of cardboard with wrapping paper and add a pretty bow. Write the words of **Luke 11:9** on the "package" as a reminder that we can trust in the good gifts God gives us.

DIRECTIONS

Before kids arrive, wrap half the gifts nicely and wrap the other half sloppily. Place all the nicely wrapped gifts in one box and all the other gifts in the second box. Display the gifts.

Say: Stand by the gifts you'd most like to receive. Ask: Why did you choose those gifts? What's the difference between these two boxes of gifts?

Give each child a gift.

Read aloud **Luke 11:9-13.** Say: All God's gifts are good, but at first some gifts may not seem as good as others. For example, your family may have to move, and you may be unhappy about it at first, but afterward you discover it's a good thing. Ask: How do God's gifts to us sometimes seem like they're wrapped in beautiful paper? yucky paper?

Say: Think about something in your life that seems like it's a yucky gift. How might it be a good gift from a loving Father?

Hold out your open hands. Let's pray. Father, help us have open hands to receive all your gifts, whether they seem good at first or not. In Jesus' name, amen.

UNCLEAN!

Kids learn about accepting others.
Text: Luke 17:11-19

WHAT YOU'LL NEED:

You'll need a Bible and large jingle bells for one-third of your children.

FOR EXTRA IMPACT:

- Play the game again, rotating positions so all children have a turn to be the lepers.

- Have kids think of a time they were left out or excluded. Help them discuss how that felt.

- Ask: What are things we can do for others who feel left out?

DIRECTIONS

Give large jingle bells to one-third of the children. Say: If you have a bell, you're a leper. You have a terrible disease called leprosy that rots away your skin. In biblical times, lepers had to cry out "Unclean!" whenever they entered a town. Everyone would run from the lepers. On "go," you lepers ring your bells, and everyone else will run from you. Anyone you touch catches your leprosy and must freeze.

After a few minutes, stop and collect the bells. Ask: How did those of you with leprosy feel? What would it feel like to be a real leper?

Read aloud **Luke 17:11-19.** Ask: What can we learn about Jesus from this Scripture? What kinds of people today are sometimes treated like lepers—no one wants to be around them? How would Jesus want us to treat those people?

Say: We can love others just as Jesus loved and accepted the lepers. Let's ask God to fill us with his love for people who aren't always accepted by others.

Close in prayer.

JESUS' FIRST MIRACLE

Kids learn about Jesus' miracles.
Text: John 2:1-11

WHAT YOU'LL NEED:

You'll need a ceramic pitcher, a clear pitcher, presweetened grape drink mix, water, a long spoon, and small clear cups. Pour the drink mix into the ceramic pitcher, and fill the clear pitcher with water.

ALLERGY ALERT
See page 10.

FOR EXTRA IMPACT:

- Read aloud **John 2:11.** Ask: Why do you think the disciples believed in Jesus when they saw the miracle he performed?

- Ask: What do you think the disciples said to each other when they saw Jesus perform this miracle? What would you have said?

- Ask: How can we show others that we have faith in Jesus?

DIRECTIONS

Say: Jesus and his friends went to a wedding party in Cana. There were so many people there that they ran out of drinks for all the guests! Jesus' mom asked Jesus to help.

Say: So Jesus walked over to six stone jars that each held more water than a bathtub. He said to the servants, "Fill these jars with water," and they did.

Pour the water into the ceramic pitcher. Stir. Say: Then Jesus said, "Pour a glass for the head of the party."

Pour the drink into a small clear cup, and show kids the new purple color. Say: Jesus changed the water, and this new drink was better than the drink that ran out! This was Jesus' first miracle! A miracle is something only God can do.

Say: Now what we did was just a trick— the drink mix was already in the ceramic pitcher. But Jesus' miracle was real. Let's thank God for Jesus' miracles—and for our good-tasting drink.

Pray, and then pour drinks for all the kids.

WORDLESS NECKLACE

Kids learn about salvation.
Text: John 3:16

WHAT YOU'LL NEED:

You'll need a 16-inch piece of red shoestring licorice and a purple, white, green, and yellow Life Savers Gummies candy (original and berry flavor) for each child.

ALLERGY ALERT
See page 10.

FOR EXTRA IMPACT:

- Read aloud **John 3:16.** Ask: How does this verse make you feel about yourself? Explain.

- Let kids each make a wordless bracelet to go along with their wordless necklaces.

- Challenge kids to wear their bracelets to school. Encourage kids to give the bracelet to the first person who asks about it and to explain to that person about God's gift of salvation.

DIRECTIONS

Have children string the purple candy onto the licorice rope. Say: As you string your purple candy onto this licorice, let it remind you of Jesus' purplish bruises caused by our sin. Jesus endured pain on the cross to pay for our sins.

Say: The red licorice reminds us that Jesus bled on the cross so we can receive God's forgiveness and eternal life.

Say: When we accept Jesus' gift of forgiveness, he washes us white as snow. String the white candy.

Say: String the green candy to remind you that God's Holy Spirit helps Christians grow in faith.

Say: When we accept Jesus' forgiveness and the gift of eternal life, we get to go to heaven when we die. String the yellow candy to remind you of heaven's streets of gold.

Have kids tie a knot in their necklace. Close in prayer.

SNACK TRICK

Kids learn about judging by appearance.
Text: John 7:24

WHAT YOU'LL NEED:

You'll need a Bible, crackers, juice, an empty cookie box, an empty milk carton, cups, and napkins.

ALLERGY ALERT
See page 10.

FOR EXTRA IMPACT:

- For each pair of kids, you'll need two identical boxes and one item small enough to fit inside one of the boxes. Let kids take turns hiding the object in one of the boxes so the other partner can guess where the object is hidden.

- Ask: How is this game like or unlike the Scripture verse?

- Ask: How did you try to make a "right judgment" about which box held the object? How is that like or unlike what God wants us to do with others?

→ DIRECTIONS

Before kids arrive, fill an empty cookie box with crackers. Fill a clean, empty milk carton with juice.

Have children sit in a circle. Have a child open the cookie box, peek in, and pass it to the right. Have all the children do the same until everyone has seen in the box.

Say: I'll pass the box around again. Take a cracker to eat as we discuss these questions. What did you think would be in this box? How did the appearance of the box fool you?

Ask: Who'd like something to drink?

When you pour juice from the carton, allow time for reactions. Then read aloud **John 7:24.** Ask: What happens when we judge people by the way they look rather than by what's inside them? How can we practice looking at the inside of a person rather than the outside? Why does Jesus say not to judge by appearances?

Let's pray. Dear God, remind us to love people who look different from us. In Jesus' name, amen.

PUTTY POWER

Kids learn about forgiveness.
Text: John 8:1-11

WHAT YOU'LL NEED:

You'll need a Bible, pencils, small paper slips, and enough Silly Putty modeling clay for everyone to have a quarter-size piece.

FOR EXTRA IMPACT:

- Give each child a piece of clay. Have kids form the clay into the shape of a heart and set it aside to dry.

- After the clay has hardened, let kids paint the clay and allow it to dry. Then have kids write "Forgiveness" in the center of the heart.

- Have kids take their clay hearts home as reminders that Jesus forgives us because he loves us.

▶ DIRECTIONS

Give each child a slip of paper, a pencil, and a piece of Silly Putty. Ask: What can this putty do?

Read aloud **John 8:1-11.** Ask: How did the Pharisees feel about the woman's sin? How did Jesus view the woman? Why is it difficult at times to ask Jesus to forgive us for our sins?

Say: On your paper slip, write a one-word sin that you need to ask Jesus to forgive. Now put your putty over the word and press hard.

Have the kids peel off the putty so the word is on it. Say: Jesus came and took all our sins on himself.

Collect the putty, and squeeze it until all the writing has disappeared. Say: When he forgives, he gives us a clean heart and holds nothing against us.

Shape the putty into a heart. Close with a prayer of thanks for forgiveness.

FOLLOW THE LEADER

Kids learn about following the real leader—Jesus!
Text: John 12:26

WHAT YOU'LL NEED:

You'll need a Bible.

FOR EXTRA IMPACT:

- Have kids lead one another in doing silly actions. Then compare how that is like or unlike how Jesus leads us.

- Have kids share ways they've followed Jesus at school or at home.

- Tell kids about a time God's leading was very clear to you.

DIRECTIONS

Play Follow the Leader several times with different leaders.

Say: Playing Follow the Leader can be lots of fun. Which do you like best—following or leading? We follow people a lot—even when we're not playing a game.

Ask: Who are people you follow? Who are people you don't want to follow? There's one person we can follow who always leads us the right way.

Read aloud **John 12:26.** Say: Jesus wants us to follow him. He loves us so much that he died and rose to save us from our sins. He's the best leader ever.

Ask: Is it always easy to follow Jesus? Why or why not? How can we help each other follow Jesus?

Pray: Thank you, Jesus, for being a leader we can always trust and follow. Amen.

THE WAY

Kids learn that Jesus is the only way to heaven.
Text: John 14:6

WHAT YOU'LL NEED:

You'll need a Bible and a plastic shape-sorter toy with a circle shape and a diamond, star, and circle hole. Draw a face on the circle shape.

FOR EXTRA IMPACT:

- Let kids each trace the diamond, star, and circle shapes on a sheet of paper. Have kids color and decorate their drawings.

- Write on each child's paper, "Jesus is the way and the truth and the life."

- Lead kids in thanking God for sending Jesus so we can live in heaven with him forever.

DIRECTIONS

Say: This puzzle is probably pretty easy for you to do. Let's pretend that this circle shape is a person.

Show the circle shape's face. Say: This person wants to get to heaven. This person decides, "I'll be a star at doing good things to get to heaven."

Have a child try to push the circle shape through the star hole.

Say: Diamonds are very costly. Can the circle say, "I'll buy my way into heaven"?

Have another child try to push the circle shape through the diamond hole. Say: Those are silly ideas! There's only one way for the circle to get into the shape-sorter. What's that one way?

Have another child push the circle shape through the circle hole. Then read aloud **John 14:6.**

Ask: How do we get to our Father in heaven? We must go through Jesus. It's that simple—just like the shape-sorter puzzle is simple. One shape, one hole. One person, one way to heaven. Jesus is the only way.

CANDY CONNECTIONS

Kids learn to find things that remind us of God.
Text: Romans 1:20

WHAT YOU'LL NEED:

You'll need a Bible and a different package of candy or candy bar for each child.

See page 10.

FOR EXTRA IMPACT:

- Let kids use their candy wrappers to make a classroom bulletin board. For example, kids could tape an Almond Joy wrapper on the board and beside it write, "God brings us joy!"

- Challenge kids to keep a list of things they find each day that remind them of their faith relationship with God. Let kids report back the following week with their discoveries.

- Have kids each tape a Bit-O-Honey candy bar onto a piece of card stock and write, "God's love is sweeter than honey!" Kids can give the cards to family members or friends.

DIRECTIONS

Give each child a different candy. Say: Analyze your candy's wrapper. What does it look like? What does it say? How is what's on your wrapper like or unlike your faith relationship with God?

Kids may discover that a package of Skittles candy has a rainbow that reminds them of God's covenant, or that all the candy has an expiration date just as we do, but God gives us eternal life.

Next have kids turn to a partner and tell what they've discovered. Then have kids tell the group the connections they discovered.

Read aloud **Romans 1:20.** Say: If we look closely enough in nature and in our world, we can find things that remind us of God. Each day this week, try to find one thing around you that reminds you of your faith relationship with God.

I CONFESS

Kids learn about God's forgiveness.
Text: Romans 3:23-26

WHAT YOU'LL NEED:

You'll need a Bible, pens, paper, pennies, and red markers.

FOR EXTRA IMPACT:

- Ask: What is grace? Why do you think God gives us his grace?

- Ask: What are things we can do to show grace to others when they hurt us or treat us wrong?

- Let kids take another red-colored penny to give to a friend and share what they've learned about God's grace and forgiveness.

▶ DIRECTIONS

Give each child five pennies. Have children sit in a circle on the floor with you.

Say: We're going to play a game called Confession. We'll go around the circle and tell something we've done wrong that we think others may have done also, such as told a lie or yelled at a friend. When you name your sin, throw a penny into the center of the circle. If anyone else has ever done that sin, throw your penny into the center of the circle also.

Continue until everyone has had a chance to name a sin. Then ask: What did you learn from this activity? What's the difference between a sin and a mistake? How can we ask God's forgiveness for our sins? How can we keep from committing the same sin again?

Read aloud **Romans 3:23-26.** Say: The Bible says we have all sinned. Take a penny and use a red marker to color one side. Keep this penny with you to remind you that Christ's blood paid for our sins. Because of Jesus' death, we can be forgiven when we ask God to forgive us.

Say: Let's pray. God, thank you for forgiving us when we sin. In Jesus' name, amen.

HOW MUCH LOVE?

Kids learn about God's love.
Text: Romans 5:8

WHAT YOU'LL NEED:

You'll need a Bible, an empty fast-food paper cup with a lid and a straw, a pitcher of water, and a pan.

FOR EXTRA IMPACT:

- Ask: Why does God want to give us more and more of his love? What happens in our lives when we accept God's love?

- Ask: Do you think being full of God's love makes it easier to show God's love to others? Explain.

- Have kids tell things they can do to show God's love to others. Challenge kids to follow through on their ideas during the week.

DIRECTIONS

Ask: How much do you think God loves you? Let's pretend this water is God's love and this cup is you.

Put the cup with a lid in the pan. Pour the water into the cup through the straw.

Say: We can act like this lid and close ourselves to God's love. If we close ourselves to God's love, we can't receive much love. How do we close ourselves to God's love?

Take off the lid and pour the water into the cup. Ask: Why is it easier for the water to get into the cup now? How can we be open to receiving God's love?

Read aloud **Romans 5:8.** Say: It's much easier if the cup is open to the water. In the same way, if we're open to God's love, we'll receive more of the love God wants to give us.

Say: Let's pray. God, thank you for loving us. Help us be open to receiving your love.

GOD'S FREE GIFT

Kids learn about eternal life.
Text: Romans 6:23

WHAT YOU'LL NEED:

You'll need a Bible, a "FREE!" sign, and a sign that says "50 Cents." You'll also need a table and inexpensive gifts such as stickers or pencils.

FOR EXTRA IMPACT:

- Give kids wrapping paper, ribbons, and bows, and let kids wrap the gifts to give to their friends.

- Have kids find partners and practice what they'll say to their friends as they tell about God's free gift.

- Have partners pray for their friends. Then thank God for his free gift of love to us all.

DIRECTIONS

Before class, put the signs at opposite ends of a table. In front of each sign, place enough gifts for all the children to have one.

Say: Who likes to get gifts? What's the best thing about a gift? Line up in front of the gift you'd like to receive on this table. Some gifts cost 50 cents and some are free.

After the children have chosen their gifts, have them sit down.

Ask: Why did you choose your gift? Is a gift really a gift if you have to pay for it? Why or why not?

Read aloud **Romans 6:23.** Say: God's gift of eternal life is FREE! We can't do anything to earn it. God wants us to share his free gift of love. Let's take another gift from the gift table and give it to a friend. When you give it to your friend, tell your friend about Jesus—God's free gift of love to us!

IT'S A MIX

Kids learn about unity in Christ.
Text: Romans 15:5-7

WHAT YOU'LL NEED:

You'll need a Bible. For each group, you'll also need vegetable oil, dark-colored vinegar, Dawn dishwashing detergent, a tablespoon, and a small jar with a lid.

FOR EXTRA IMPACT:

- Ask: Why is it so hard to be excluded? Explain. What would Jesus think of excluding others?

- Ask: How can knowing that Jesus accepts you change how you treat others? Explain.

- Ask: How does accepting others glorify God?

DIRECTIONS

Form groups of four. Have one child in each group pour a small amount of oil into the jar.

Have a second child in each group add more oil, replace the lid, and shake the jar. Say: When we poured more oil in the jar, it mixed just fine.

Have a third child from each group add a tablespoon of vinegar to the jar, replace the lid, and shake. (The oil and vinegar don't mix.)

Ask: What happened to the mixture in the jar? When we meet someone different from us, we might think, "This person is just too different. How can we get along?" If we don't accept people, we'll never mix—or get along.

Say: Let's add a few drops of dishwashing soap and see what happens.

Have a fourth child from each group add soap, replace the lid, and shake. (The oil and vinegar mix.)

Read aloud **Romans 15:5-7.** Ask: How is Jesus like the dishwashing soap? How does Jesus make the difference in helping us accept others?

Say: Let's pray. Lord, thank you for accepting us. Help us accept others. In Jesus' name, amen.

ABOUT TO POP

Kids learn about conflict.
Text: 1 Corinthians 1:10

WHAT YOU'LL NEED:
You'll need a Bible and large rubber bands.

FOR EXTRA IMPACT:

- Give each team of four four inflated balloons. Give kids time to plan, and then have teams race to pop their balloons the fastest.

- Say: The Bible tells us that we are to be "perfectly united in mind and thought." How is that like or unlike working together in our balloon popping game?

- Ask: Why does God want us to be united in mind and thought?

DIRECTIONS

Form pairs, and have partners face each other. Give each pair a rubber band.

Say: With your partner, hold onto each end of your rubber band. I'll make several statements that could hurt a friendship. If you think those things would damage a friendship, take a step back and still hold onto the rubber band.

Here are the statements:

Your friend said she'd call you after school, but she didn't.

You were goofing off with friends, and one of them got rough and pushed you.

One of your friends is always making fun of you in class.

Your friend called you a bad name.

A friend got mad at you and let the air out of your bike tires.

Ask: What has happened to your rubber band? What would happen to it if I kept listing hurtful things?

Read aloud **1 Corinthians 1:10.** Ask: What did Paul tell people to do to resolve their conflicts? How does conflict affect your friendships? How can you resolve conflict in your friendships?

OUT OF CONTROL

Kids learn about drug abuse.
Text: 1 Corinthians 6:19-20

WHAT YOU'LL NEED:

You'll need a Bible and masking tape.

FOR EXTRA IMPACT:

- Have partners share with the class their ideas on how to respond if offered drugs or alcohol.

- Let partners choose an idea, then role-play using that idea.

- Ask: How was your idea like or unlike honoring God with your body? How do you think God feels when we honor him with our bodies? when we don't?

DIRECTIONS

Before kids arrive, mark several straight lines on the floor with masking tape.

Say: Let's see how straight and tall you can walk on these lines.

Have children take turns walking along the tape lines. Then ask: What was it like to walk along the lines?

Say: Let's walk the lines again, but with a twist. Everyone stand up and spread out so you have plenty of room. Now twirl around six or seven times. Walk along the lines right after you twirl.

Let children walk along the lines. Then have them sit down, and ask: What was it like to walk the line after you twirled around? How was it the same or different from the first time you walked the line?

Say: Even something as easy as walking a straight line becomes hard when our senses are impaired. When people use drugs or alcohol, it's hard for them to think clearly, just as it was hard for you to walk the line after you twirled around.

Read aloud **1 Corinthians 6:19-20.**
Say: God wants us to use our bodies to honor him. Turn to a partner, and tell that person what you'll do if anyone ever offers you drugs or alcohol.

Close in prayer.

PRESSURE POT

Kids learn about peer pressure.
Text: 1 Corinthians 15:33

WHAT YOU'LL NEED:

You'll need a Bible.

FOR EXTRA IMPACT:

- Ask: Why do you think the Bible says that "bad company corrupts good character"? What does "good character" mean?

- Have kids find partners, and let them take turns playing the clapping game.

- Have partners talk about specific examples of positive peer pressure. Challenge kids to use those examples in their everyday lives.

DIRECTIONS

Have an adult take a volunteer to a place where he or she can't hear what you say.

Say: When the volunteer comes back, we're going to try to get the volunteer to scratch his or her head. We'll begin by clapping slowly, and as our volunteer gets close to doing what we want, we'll start clapping faster. If the volunteer is far from doing what we want, we'll clap slower.

Call the volunteer back. Say: These people are going to help you do something. You have to figure out what that something is. They won't speak, but they'll clap. The faster the clapping, the closer you are to doing what they want. Let's go.

After the volunteer figures out the action or after three minutes, call time. Ask: How did you feel as people tried to get you to do something? How did the rest of you feel trying to get our volunteer to do something? How do you feel when kids try to get you to do something you don't want to do?

Read aloud **1 Corinthians 15:33.** Ask: What does this verse say about peer pressure? Can peer pressure be good? Explain. How can we not give in to negative peer pressure?

Say: Let's pray. God, help us choose our friends wisely. And please help us stand strong against negative peer pressure. In Jesus' name, amen.

MAGNETIC APPEAL

Kids learn about becoming like Jesus.
Text: 2 Corinthians 3:18

WHAT YOU'LL NEED:

You'll need a Bible, a bar magnet, a nail, and paper clips. Due to the varying power of magnets, try this ahead of time to determine how long the nail needs to be exposed to the magnet.

FOR EXTRA IMPACT:

- Have kids find partners, and let pairs try to magnetize a nail and pick up paper clips.

- Ask: How is the nail becoming magnetized like or unlike what happens to us when we are changed into Christ's likeness?

- Lead kids in asking for God's transformation in their lives.

DIRECTIONS

Have kids use the magnet to pick up the paper clips and the nail. Ask: What are magnets used for?

Have children try to pick up a paper clip with the nail. Ask: Why can't you do it? This nail and the paper clips are both made out of metals that cling to magnets, but the metals don't cling to each other. For the metals to cling together, one of them has to be changed.

Stroke the nail in one direction over the bar magnet about 40 times. Then pick up a paper clip with the nail. Ask: How did that happen? The nail was magnetized—transformed by its contact with the magnet.

Read aloud **2 Corinthians 3:18.** Ask: How do you think Christians are transformed into the likeness of Christ? In what ways would you like to become more like Christ?

CELEBRATE NEW LIFE

Kids celebrate new life in Jesus!
Text: 2 Corinthians 5:17

NEW TESTAMENT

WHAT YOU'LL NEED:

You'll need a Bible, banners, party hats, noisemakers, streamers, praise music, and a music player.

FOR EXTRA IMPACT:

- Bring in pictures or actual caterpillars and butterflies, and talk about how caterpillars become butterflies. Ask: How is that like or unlike what happens when we become new creations in Christ?

- Have kids make butterflies by painting coffee filters with watercolors and then cinching the filter in the middle when dry. Add a chenille wire for the antennae, and clip together with a clothespin. Attach a card that says, "I'm a new creation in Christ!"

DIRECTIONS

Ask: How many of you like parades? Say: Parades are a chance to celebrate a person or a holiday. On New Year's Day, we celebrate a new year and a fresh start for our lives.

Say: Jesus tells us in his Word that he offers us new life in him.

Read aloud **2 Corinthians 5:17.** Say: That's something to celebrate! Let's have a celebration parade to celebrate the new life we have in Jesus.

Have the children hold banners, wear hats, blow noisemakers, or carry streamers as they march around the room. Encourage kids to praise Jesus with phrases such as, "Yea, Jesus!" or "Jesus, you're awesome!" As kids march around, play praise music. After the parade, have kids stand around you.

Ask: How do we receive this new life in Jesus? How can we share this new life with others this year?

Say: Let's pray. Thank you, Lord, for loving us enough to give us a new life in you. Help us to share this good news with our friends. In Jesus' name, amen.

SET FREE

Kids learn about God's mercy.
Text: Galatians 5:1

WHAT YOU'LL NEED:

You'll need a Bible. For each child, you'll need a paper grocery bag and 3 to 4 heavy objects, such as bricks, large rocks, or filled gallon jugs.

FOR EXTRA IMPACT:

- Ask: What are things we can do to stand firm and resist the temptation of sin?

- Have kids each paint a large red heart on their paper bags. When dry, let kids write, "Jesus sets me free."

- Let kids silently thank God for the freedom they have in Jesus.

DIRECTIONS

Say: Sins are things we do that are wrong. Think about your sins from this last week. As you think of each one, silently pick up a heavy object and put it in a bag.

Allow time for everyone to fill a bag. Then say: Let's see how it feels to carry our sins with us on a walk around our room. Carry your bag until I say you can put it down. If something falls out, stop and pick it up.

After three minutes, go to one child, take the bag away, set it down, and whisper the first part of **Galatians 5:1**—"It is for freedom that Christ has set us free." Continue until all the children are set free.

Ask: How did you feel when you were carrying these heavy objects for your sins? How is carrying these heavy objects like or unlike carrying your sins around with you? How did you feel when I took your bag from you? How is removing the bags like or unlike what Christ did for us on the cross?

GOD'S ARMOR

Kids learn how to defend themselves against temptation.
Text: Ephesians 6:10-17

WHAT YOU'LL NEED:

You'll need a Bible.

FOR EXTRA IMPACT:

- Ask: Why do you think God tells us how to protect ourselves from temptation?

- Give kids each card stock cut in the shape of a shield. Let kids write on their shields, "I have God's armor to be strong in the Lord."

- Give kids a copy of the motions. Encourage kids to teach the motions to their family members.

DIRECTIONS

Ask: What's temptation? When are you tempted? How can we defend ourselves against attacks of temptation?

Read aloud **Ephesians 6:10-17.** Have everyone stand. Say: We need to put on God's armor when we're attacked by temptation. To remember this, I'll say a phrase and do a motion. You repeat the phrase and imitate the motion.

Belt of truth—put hands on hips. Say, "No lies."

Breastplate of righteousness—beat chest. Say, "Good deeds."

Shoes—stomp feet. Say, "Stomp the devil."

Shield of faith—cross arms across chest. say, "Have faith."

Helmet of salvation—put hands on head, Say, "I'm protected."

Sword of the Spirit—hands as an open book. Say, "God's Word."

When kids know the motions, try some of these options: saying phrases faster and faster, calling out the armor and letting kids respond with the motion, calling pieces out of order, and doing the motions and letting kids call out the correct piece of armor.

Pray: God, thank you for providing your armor when we're tempted to do the wrong thing. In Jesus' name, amen.

TRADING CARDS

Kids learn about praying for others.
Text: Ephesians 6:18

WHAT YOU'LL NEED:

Using tag board, cut 2 trading cards for each child. You'll also need pens and a Bible.

FOR EXTRA IMPACT:

- Bring in a Polaroid or digital camera with printer, and let kids glue actual photographs onto their trading cards.

- The following week, have kids write a note of encouragement or draw a picture to give to their prayer partners to let them know they're being prayed for.

- After a few weeks, let kids report back with any praise reports of answered prayers.

▶ DIRECTIONS

Give each child two cards. Have kids draw a self-portrait on the front of each card and autograph it. Have kids write their name, age, and a prayer request on the back of each card. Explain that others will be reading their requests.

Read aloud **Ephesians 6:18.** Say: Walk around the room and trade cards with each other until I tell you to stop. You need to trade cards with at least three different people. As you trade, keep in mind that you will be praying for the people whose cards you end up with.

Call time after one minute.

Say: Let the people know that you have their cards. Remember to pray for each other in the next few weeks. Put your cards somewhere you'll see them every day.

GOAL TENDERS

Kids learn to strive for God's best.
Text: Philippians 3:12-14

NEW TESTAMENT

WHAT YOU'LL NEED:

You'll need a Bible, empty bowls, and buttons.

FOR EXTRA IMPACT:

- Let older kids write the words of **Philippians 13:14** on a piece of card stock. Write the words for younger kids.

- Have kids write their goal of becoming what God wants them to be on the back of their cards. Help younger kids write, or let them draw pictures.

- Let kids glue buttons on the cards for decoration. Punch a hole in the top of each card, and add a ribbon for a hanger. Encourage kids to hang the cards in their rooms to remind them to strive to follow God.

DIRECTIONS

Form trios, and give each group an empty bowl and a handful of buttons.

Say: On New Year's Day, many people set goals to achieve in the coming year.

Hold up an empty bowl. Say: This bowl reminds me of an empty new year, ready to be filled with new experiences, activities, and people. Let's pretend your buttons represent all those fun things.

Say: Your goal is to toss your buttons into the empty bowl from three feet away.

After two minutes, collect the bowls. Ask: Were you able to achieve your goal and toss a button into the bowl each time?

Say: In life, sometimes you have to try several times to achieve your goals. But God gives us each a special goal to strive for every day, week, month, and year.

Read aloud **Philippians 3:12-14.**

Say: Our goal is to become what God wants us to be.

Place a bowl in the middle of the group. Say: As we close, toss a button into this bowl. As you do, think of one way you'll try to become what God wants you to be. Maybe you'll read your Bible, pray, or show love to others.

PRAYER CHAIN

Kids learn to pray for others.
Text: Colossians 1:9

WHAT YOU'LL NEED:

You'll need ten 6x1-inch different-color paper strips, a marker, and clear tape for each team.

FOR EXTRA IMPACT:

- Give kids extra loops so they can write more prayer requests or praises of thanksgiving. Let them take their prayer chains home to hang in their rooms as reminders to pray for their friends daily.

- Ask: Why should we pray for our friends? Why do you think God wants us to pray for each other?

- Have kids find partners and share prayer requests. Encourage partners to pray for each other during the week.

DIRECTIONS

Form two teams, and give each team its supplies. Say: Today we're going to make prayer chains. On "go," write a person's name and a prayer request on each strip. It's OK if one person has more than one strip. Connect your loops to make a chain with the prayers to the outside.

After teams finish, have them stand and hold their chains. Read aloud **Colossians 1:9.** Then have kids trade chains and pray for at least two of the requests as a team.

Afterward, have kids each take home at least one loop to pray for that person during the week. Kids may need to take more than one loop to make sure all the loops are taken.

SALTY SPEECH

Kids learn about wholesome speech.
Text: Colossians 4:6

NEW TESTAMENT

WHAT YOU'LL NEED:

You'll need a Bible, salt-free pretzels, and regular pretzels.

ALLERGY ALERT
See page 10.

FOR EXTRA IMPACT:

- Let kids eat pretzel-and-cheese snacks. As kids eat, have them tell examples of unsalty conversation.
- Ask: How does unsalty conversation make someone feel? Explain. How does salty conversation make someone feel? Explain.
- Ask: Why does God want us to keep our conversations full of grace?

DIRECTIONS

Read aloud **Colossians 4:6.** Say: Let's discover the difference between the kind of conversation Paul called salty and the kind that isn't full of grace.

Have children nibble each kind of pretzel. Ask: Which pretzel tasted more "seasoned with salt"? How would you describe the other pretzel?

Say: The main ingredient is the same in both pretzels, but one is salty. Salt makes us thirsty.

Say: Two different conversations may have the same main ingredient, such as talking about someone. How could one conversation be salty, filled with grace, and pleasing to God? How could that same conversation be unsalty, empty of grace, and unpleasing to God?

Encourage children to discuss tone of voice, gentle words, and avoiding put-down humor. Close in prayer, asking God to make children's speech salty and pleasing.

CHILDREN AS LEADERS

Kids learn about being a good example.
Text: 1 Timothy 4:11-14

WHAT YOU'LL NEED:

You'll need a Bible, a blindfold, and an open area outside or in your classroom. (Be sure the area is free of table corners, steps, or other obstacles.)

FOR EXTRA IMPACT:

- Have kids list specific ways they can be good leaders at school.

- Challenge kids to pick one thing they can do to set an example for others at school, and one they can do at home.

- Pray: Lord, help us to be examples of your love to others in all that we say and do. In Jesus' name, amen.

DIRECTIONS

Pick one child in the group to be the Leader. Have everyone line up behind that child. Put a blindfold on the Leader. Play Follow the Leader where the Leader walks around the room and changes his or her motions as the rest of the class follows. Allow another child to be the Leader if time permits.

Ask: Leader, how did you feel as you led? Did you believe the others were doing what you were doing? Did you have any clues about what they were doing? We need to remember that the way we act can be a good or bad example for others, but we can't change others' behavior.

Read aloud **1 Timothy 4:11-14.** Ask: How can we be leaders in our homes? What are some ways that we can serve God and be leaders in our church? How can we be leaders in speech? conduct? love? faith?

FIVE KERNELS

Kids learn that God provides for all our needs.
Text: 1 Timothy 6:17

WHAT YOU'LL NEED:

You'll need a Bible and 5 kernels of candy corn in a sandwich bag tied closed with a fall-colored ribbon for each child.

See page 10.

FOR EXTRA IMPACT:

- Read aloud **1 Timothy 6:17.** Ask: Why should we put our hope in God?

- Ask: Why do you think God wants to provide for all our needs?

- Let kids make candy corn bundles to share with friends or family members. Encourage kids to tell others about God's love and provision.

DIRECTIONS

Say: The first winter the pilgrims spent in America was very cold. Some days, all they had was just enough for each person to have only five kernels of corn. When spring came, the pilgrims planted their corn, and it grew so they had a lot of food the next year. From that time on at Thanksgiving, the pilgrims each kept five kernels of corn at their plates to remind them of God's provision.

Give each child a bag of candy corn. Say: This candy corn reminds us of how God takes care of us, too.

Hold up each kernel as you read the following:

The first kernel reminds us that God loves us.

The second kernel reminds us that God provides for all our needs.

The third kernel reminds us of the friends God has given us—just as the Native Americans were friends to the pilgrims.

The fourth kernel reminds us of all the people God has given us who love us.

And the fifth kernel reminds us that God hears our prayers and answers us.

Say: Let's pray. God, thank you for providing for all our needs and for loving us. We love you. In Jesus' name, amen.

GRAB BAG

Kids learn about the purpose of Scripture.
Text: 2 Timothy 3:16-17

WHAT YOU'LL NEED:

You'll need a Bible and a bag of objects, such as a hammer, a hand mixer, makeup, and a car key.

FOR EXTRA IMPACT:

- Ask: How does God give us what we need to do the good works he wants us to do?

- Ask: How do you think God feels when we do good works for him? How does doing things for God help others believe in him?

- Challenge kids to spend time reading their Bibles during the week. Have kids report back what they learned.

DIRECTIONS

Have children each take an object out of the bag and tell what it is. Have them each demonstrate how their object is used and tell how that task could be done without the object. After everyone has had a turn, show the children a Bible. Ask: What is this? What is it used for?

Read aloud **2 Timothy 3:16-17** in an easy-to-understand translation such as the Hands-On Bible. Ask: What do these verses say the Bible is used for? One reason that God has given us Scripture is so we can know the good things he wants us to do. What are some good things God wants us to do? If you didn't have a Bible, how would you know what to do for God? How can we use our Bibles this week to learn what God wants?

Close in a prayer of thanks for Scripture and the opportunity to have Bibles.

TEACH ME

Kids learn about telling others about Jesus.
Text: 2 Timothy 4:2-4

WHAT YOU'LL NEED:

You'll need a Bible, a loaf of bread, softened cream cheese, a knife, jelly, napkins, paper, and pencils.

ALLERGY ALERT
See page 10.

FOR EXTRA IMPACT:

- Let kids make their own cream cheese and jelly sandwiches to eat for snack. As kids enjoy their sandwiches, have them each think of someone they can tell about Jesus.

- Let kids practice with partners what they will say about Jesus.

- Challenge kids to tell their friends how to follow Jesus. Let kids report back the next week.

DIRECTIONS

Form two groups. Have one group write directions for making a cream cheese and jelly sandwich. Collect the instructions, and have the other group follow them explicitly. If the instructions leave out anything, such as spreading the cream cheese with a knife, group members must use their fingers to spread.

Read aloud **2 Timothy 4:2-4.** Ask: What worked the way you planned with your instructions? What went wrong? How is making this sandwich like or unlike telling people about Jesus? What instructions would you give a person about how to follow Jesus?

Let's pray. Please help us, God, to give clear instructions to people who need to know about Jesus. In Jesus' name, amen.

HANG ON!

Kids learn about God's faithfulness.
Text: Titus 1:2

WHAT YOU'LL NEED:

You'll need a Bible, a sturdy rope, and an adult volunteer.

FOR EXTRA IMPACT:

- Ask: What does it mean to keep a promise? What happens when you don't keep a promise?

- Ask: Why do you think God always keeps his promises to us? Why should we keep our promises to others?

- Give each child a small piece of rope as a reminder that God always keeps his promises.

DIRECTIONS

Ask: Have you ever made a promise? Why is it important to keep promises?

With the volunteer, take opposite ends of the rope. Say: I promise I won't let go. Will you promise? Let's lean back and hold on.

Ask children: What if I break my promise? What would you think of me if I let go right now? Do you want to try this?

Have children promise to hold on as they lean back.

Say: If you had to hold this rope forever, you'd want someone who'd be able to keep his or her promise. Who always keeps a promise? What promises does God make? Does God ever lie?

Paraphrase **Titus 1:2.** Ask: What does it mean that God does not lie? How do you feel knowing that God always tells the truth? God keeps all his promises. He'll never let go of us. Let's thank God for keeping all his promises.

Close with a short prayer.

EGGSTRA SOFT HEARTS

NEW TESTAMENT

Kids learn about hardened hearts.
Text: Hebrews 3:7-12

WHAT YOU'LL NEED:

You'll need a Bible, 6 hard-boiled eggs and 6 raw eggs in an egg carton, and a clear bowl.

FOR EXTRA IMPACT:

- Give kids flat rocks and markers. Have kids write on each rock a different thing that can make our hearts hard, such as not forgiving, bitterness, or anger.

- Ask: Do you want to hold onto your rock? Why or Why not? How is that like or unlike holding onto a hard heart?

- Have kids exchange the rocks for heart stickers.

DIRECTIONS

Ask a child to crack any egg into the clear bowl. Then ask another child to crack an egg, and continue until at least one raw egg and one hard-boiled egg have been cracked.

Say: When you boil an egg, a change happens inside to make the egg harden. We couldn't make cookies with the hard-boiled eggs—they're too hard, and the cookies wouldn't taste very good!

Read aloud **Hebrews 3:7-12.** Say: When we read the Bible but ignore what God says, our hearts harden a little bit. We turn away from God. But when we listen to God and keep our hearts soft, he can do sweet things through us!

Say: Think for a moment about how your heart might be hard or soft. Turn to a partner, and pray together that God will make all our hearts soft.

FILL 'ER UP

Kids learn about encouraging others.
Text: Hebrews 3:13

WHAT YOU'LL NEED:

You'll need a Bible and an audible signal, such as a whistle.

FOR EXTRA IMPACT:

- Ask: Why does God want us to encourage others? What is it like to get encouragement? How does that change the way you feel about what you're doing?

- Have kids write an encouraging note or draw a picture for a friend or family member.

- Challenge kids to try to encourage another person at least once a day during the coming week.

DIRECTIONS

Form pairs. Tell kids they have 15 seconds to say something encouraging to their partners. On your signal, they'll find new partners and have another 15 seconds to encourage their new partners. Use your signal four times to mark every 15 seconds. If kids know each other well, tell them they have to comment on more than physical appearances.

Ask: How did it feel when someone encouraged you? when you encouraged others?

Read aloud **Hebrews 3:13.** Ask: How do you think encouragement can keep people's hearts soft? When does God want us to encourage others?

Say: Think of someone you know who you can encourage today. Let's pray. Dear God, help us to be people who give courage to others by our encouragement. Amen.

WHAT DO YOU SAY?

Kids learn about peer pressure.
Text: Hebrews 10:24-25

WHAT YOU'LL NEED:

You'll need a Bible and two $1 bills.

FOR EXTRA IMPACT:

- Ask: What are ways we can encourage and support each other? Why does God want us to help one another?

- Encourage kids to choose one idea and implement that idea during the week to support or encourage another person.

- Have kids report back the following week about how their encouragement was received. Ask: What was it like to help others?

DIRECTIONS

Ask a volunteer to stand beside you and be the "player" in this game. Say: I'm going to give you one dollar. Decide what special thing you'd like to do with this money. You have one minute to think about your answer. The other kids will yell out suggestions. If you choose another person's answer, that person will get one dollar. If you don't listen to someone else's answer, then no one else gets a dollar.

Allow one minute for kids to play.

Ask: What's your answer? Did anyone influence your decision? Why or why not?

If the child was influenced, have the player name only one person. Then take the dollar from the player and give it to the child who influenced him or her.

Ask: How did you feel as people pressured you to give their answers? How did the rest of you feel as you pressured the player? How did you feel when you lost or kept the dollar?

Read aloud **Hebrews 10:24-25.** Ask: According to this Scripture, how can we use peer pressure in a positive way to influence others for good?

BELIEVING IS SEEING

Kids learn about faith.
Text: Hebrews 11:1, 6

WHAT YOU'LL NEED:

You'll need a Bible, a knife, and an apple in a brown paper lunch bag.

ALLERGY ALERT
See page 10.

FOR EXTRA IMPACT:

- Provide apple wedges for a snack. As kids eat, have them tell actions that can please God.

- Ask: Why is it important to please God? Why do you think God rewards those who seek him?

- Give each child an apple to take home as a reminder of God's faithfulness.

DIRECTIONS

Say: I have something in this bag that no human eye has ever seen nor human hand touched. Do you believe me? For those of you who believe me, why do you believe me? Why do some of you not believe me?

Say: Let's see if I'm telling the truth.

Take out the apple and slice it in half. Show kids the apples seeds that no one has ever seen or touched.

Say: Many of you believed me because of the relationship that you have with me. I've never lied to you before, so you had faith in me.

Say: In the same way, the better we know God, the more we'll trust him. As we see that God is always faithful and never lies, we'll believe that everything he says in the Bible is true.

Read aloud **Hebrews 11:1, 6.**

Say: Let's pray. Dear God, we praise you because everything you say is true. Thank you that we can trust you totally. In Jesus' name, amen.

BELIEVING THE IMPOSSIBLE

NEW TESTAMENT

Kids learn about faith.
Text: Hebrews 11:6

WHAT YOU'LL NEED:

You'll need a Bible; a large, lightweight ball; and a small wastebasket. The ball must be too large to fit into the wastebasket.

FOR EXTRA IMPACT:

- List kids' prayer needs, and hang the list in your classroom.

- Have kids form groups of three and in their groups choose one or two prayer requests from the list. Let kids pray for those requests at the beginning of each class, and encourage kids to pray for those needs on their own.

- Have kids report to the class as prayer requests are answered, and mark the prayer list as a visible reminder that God helps us.

DIRECTIONS

Ask: Who would like to try to shoot this ball into this basket?

Have the child who volunteers stand 10 feet from the basket and shoot. Give the child two or three chances.

Ask: Why won't the ball go into the basket? That's right! The ball is bigger than the basket.

Lay the ball on the basket opening. Say: It's impossible for this big ball to fit into that little basket.

Ask: How many of you want to please God? Did you know that it's impossible to please God without having something? What do you think we need to have to please God?

Read aloud **Hebrews 11:6.** Say: Faith is believing that God can do the impossible. What is something that you've thought is impossible for God to help you with? Let's pray that God will help us with these problems that are too big for us to handle alone.

Close in prayer for kids' needs.

PRESIDENTIAL PRAYERS

Kids learn about obeying our leaders.
Text: Hebrews 13:17

WHAT YOU'LL NEED:

You'll need a Bible and 1 paper dollar and 1 coin for each child.

FOR EXTRA IMPACT:

- Ask: Who are other "leaders" in your life? How do they keep watch over you?

- Let kids make coin rubbings by placing different coins under newsprint. Have kids carefully rub over the coins with crayons.

- Have kids write, "'Obey your leaders and submit to their authority'—Hebrews 13:17" at the top of their papers. Tell kids to take the rubbings home to remind them to pray for our leaders.

DIRECTIONS

Give each child a coin (a penny, nickel, dime, or quarter). Say: Look at your coin, and tell me what you see on each side. These presidents have led our country through wars, decisions, and difficulties. On Presidents' Day, we celebrate these men and the others who've been our country's leaders.

Hold up the paper dollar. Say: Since I have the dollar, I'll be the leader today. Follow my instructions. If you have a quarter, do 10 jumping jacks. If you have a nickel, stand up and shout, "Nickel, nickel, buy me a pickle!" If you have a penny, shake someone hand. If you have a dime, hop around our group.

After two minutes, have children sit. Say: I sure gave you some silly instructions to follow. In fact, you might not have wanted to obey me! Even though real presidents don't tell us to do such silly things, sometimes people don't want to obey them either. But the Bible tells us to obey our leaders.

Read aloud **Hebrews 13:17.** Ask: Why is it important to obey our leaders? What would happen if no one obeyed the president?

Say: Let's pray. Find the others who have a coin like yours. Together, pray for our leaders.

BALLOON FAITH

Kids learn about forgiveness.
Text: 1 John 1:9

WHAT YOU'LL NEED:

You'll need 1 large red balloon and 1 medium yellow balloon for each child. You'll also need transparent tape, a long pin, and a Bible.

FOR EXTRA IMPACT:

- Have kids think of specific sins they've committed and silently confess them to God.

- Pray together: Lord, we confess our sins to you today and ask you to forgive us and cleanse our hearts. In Jesus' name, amen.

- Have kids use markers to write, "God forgives" on their red balloons. Let kids take their balloons home as reminders of God's faithfulness to forgive our sins.

DIRECTIONS

Give a red balloon, a yellow balloon, and a piece of tape to each child. Say: Let's imagine that this yellow balloon is our sin—the things we've done to disobey God or hurt other people. How do you feel when you sin? We're going to see how God forgives and forgets our sin.

Say: Insert the yellow balloon inside the red balloon, keeping both openings together. Inflate them at the same time. The red balloon represents Jesus' blood.

Have kids stop inflating before the balloons get too large, and then show them how to tie off both balloons at once. Have each child carefully place a piece of tape on the red balloon.

Read aloud **1 John 1:9.** Say: Now, let's close our eyes and ask God to forgive our sin.

After children pray, help each child push the pin through the tape to pop the yellow balloon. The red balloon will stay inflated.

Ask: What happened to the yellow balloon that represents our sin? How is the yellow balloon like our sin after we ask for forgiveness?

LIVING VALENTINES

Kids learn about showing love with action and truth.
Text: 1 John 3:18

WHAT YOU'LL NEED:

You'll need a Bible and conversation hearts candies.

ALLERGY ALERT
See page 10.

FOR EXTRA IMPACT:

- Have kids make valentine cards with craft supplies such as paper doilies, ribbons, stickers, and lace. Help kids send the cards to military personnel overseas.

- Have kids fill small snack-size zipper bags with candy hearts and tie with red and pink ribbon. Give the treats to children at a local women's shelter.

- Have kids decorate heart-shaped cookies with frosting and candy decorations. Wrap in plastic wrap, tie with pretty ribbon, and give to your church's shut-ins to show they're remembered.

DIRECTIONS

Ask: What special things do you do to celebrate Valentine's Day?

Give each child a candy. Have kids turn to a partner and tell that person the message on their candy. Help early readers with the messages.

Say: It's great to give each other special messages, but the Bible talks about another way we can show love to each other.

Read aloud **1 John 3:18.** Ask: What does this verse say to do to show our love? How can we show love with our actions? Who could you show love to this week?

Say: Let's practice loving actions right now. Here are two heart-shaped candies for each of you.

Pass out the candies. Have kids give one of their candies to someone else, then give that person a hug and say, "Jesus loves you." Tell kids to keep the other candy to remind them to show love to people this week. Then close in prayer.

LOVE-LETTER PUPPET SKIT

Kids learn about God's love.
Text: 1 John 4:9-12

WHAT YOU'LL NEED:

You'll need a Bible, a chipmunk puppet, and a heart-shaped box.

FOR EXTRA IMPACT:

- Let kids use socks, yarn, markers, glue, and ribbon to make their own sock puppets.
- Have kids form groups of three or four, and let each group come up with a short puppet skit to show God's love.
- Have groups perform their skits for the class.

▶ DIRECTIONS

Chadwick: I'm in love! I'm in love!

Leader: Tell us what she looks like.

Chadwick: I wrote a poem about her: Her eyes are like stars that glisten at night. Her hair is like velvet: oh, what a sight.

Leader: Will you give her the poem?

Chadwick: No, but I'll write her a love letter. *(To children)* Will you help me?

Leader: Sure. Have you started yet?

Chadwick: Dearest darling, I, Chadwick Chester Chipmunk III…That's as far as I've gotten. What should I put next?

Leader: I love you.

Chadwick: Oh, I love you, too.

Leader: I mean, why don't you tell her you love her? *(To children)* What else should Chadwick tell his sweetheart?

Leader: God has sent a love letter to *you!* *(Open a heart-shaped candy box to reveal a Bible inside. Read aloud 1 John 4:9-12.)* God loves you very much. Let's thank God for loving us so much.

Close in prayer.

SHARING YOUR HEART

Kids learn that God wants us to love others.
Text: 1 John 4:10-11

WHAT YOU'LL NEED:

You'll need a Bible and 8½x11-inch sheets of red paper.

FOR EXTRA IMPACT:

- Give kids construction paper and craft supplies, and let kids make and decorate additional hearts for their friends and family members.

- Give kids conversation heart candies for a snack. As kids eat the treats, have kids tell ways that God shows he loves us.

- Encourage kids to share their heart candies with someone special and tell that special person about God's love.

DIRECTIONS

Give kids each a sheet of red paper. As you tell the following story, have them do the steps along with you.

Say: Today we're going to use our red papers to tell a story about a girl who didn't get any valentines at school. Ask: How do you think she felt?

Say: This girl was so sad she decided to take a walk in a large meadow with red spring flowers. *(Hold up your paper and encourage others to do as you do.)*

She came to a small garden of red tulips. *(Fold your paper in half lengthwise.)* She felt tired and lay down. She put some flowers over her as a blanket. *(Fold a bottom corner up.)*

When she awoke, she saw an arrow. *(Fold the other bottom corner back.)* The arrow was pointing to a curving stream. *(Tear a rounded corner off the top.)* As she walked to the stream, she got very excited and happy because she remembered something she learned in church.

Read aloud **1 John 4:10-11.**

Say: She ran home and made valentines for all her friends so she could share the great love God had given to her. *(Open the paper to reveal a heart.)*

This week, share God's love with as many people as possible. Give your heart to someone you care about.

A HOME IN HEAVEN

Kids learn about heaven.
Text: Revelation 21:1-4; 21:22–22:5

WHAT YOU'LL NEED:

You'll need a Bible, a box of tissues, an adhesive bandage, an aspirin bottle, a night light, a key, and a bottle of water.

FOR EXTRA IMPACT:

- Read aloud **Revelation 22:3-5.** Ask: What do you think it means that God's name will be on our foreheads?

- Have kids turn to a partner, give a high five, and say, "You can be God's child forever."

- Ask: What do you think heaven will be like?

DIRECTIONS

Say: When Jesus was here on earth he told his disciples a little about heaven. He said that anyone could live there with him if they were a part of his family.

Say: I brought some things today we don't need in heaven.

Hold up the box of tissues. Ask: What do you use a tissue for? Why won't we need a tissue in heaven? The Bible says that no one will cry in heaven. (Read aloud **Revelation 21:4a.**)

Read the related Scriptures as you follow this pattern with the remaining props. Bandage and aspirin—no pain in heaven, **Revelation 21:4b;** night light—God will be our light, **Revelation 21:23;** key—gates will never be shut, **Revelation 21:25;** bottle of water—the River of Life flows from God's throne, **Revelation 22:1-2.**

Say: Just as we live in our family's house here on earth, Jesus wants us to be a part of his family and live in heaven with him.

Share with children how they can become a part of God's family. Close in prayer thanking God for creating a great place for our future home.

SMILE BIG

Kids learn about joy.
Text: Revelation 21:3-4

WHAT YOU'LL NEED:

You'll need a Bible, happy-face stickers, and an instant-print camera.

ALLERGY ALERT
See page 10.

FOR EXTRA IMPACT:

- Let kids make smiley-face fruit snacks by using an apple slice for a mouth, grape halves for eyes, and a banana slice for the nose.

- As kids eat their smiley-face snacks, encourage them to say things that make them happy. Then let kids think of ways to make others happy.

- Take each child's picture, and hang it on a bulletin board. Write, "Jesus makes me smile," above the pictures. Let kids write their names under their pictures.

DIRECTIONS

Say: The Bible says that a happy heart makes your face cheerful.

Lead children in singing "If You're Happy and You Know It." Include a completion verse that says, "Smile big!"

Say: If I were about to take a picture of you, what would you do with your mouth? Yes, you'd smile for the camera.

Take an instant-print shot of children and then pass it around to kids.

Ask: Why do people smile? When we smile for pictures and other times, we're showing on the outside that we're really happy on the inside.

Ask: Why are people happy on the inside? What do Christians have to be happy about?

Say: We have a lot to be happy about; we can smile real big.

Read aloud **Revelation 21:3-4.** Say: Since we'll be smiling in heaven forever, let's spend this whole week practicing! Not only will it make us feel better, but it'll brighten everyone else's day, too. Tell people that Jesus is the reason for your smile.

Give each child a happy-face sticker.

NEW TESTAMENT

REAL A-PEEL

Kids learn about bearing good fruit.
Text: Matthew 7:17-20

WHAT YOU'LL NEED:

You'll need a Bible, a toothpick, and a banana.

ALLERGY ALERT
See page 10.

FOR EXTRA IMPACT:

- Cut apples in half from top to bottom. Let kids dip an apple half in red paint and then press it onto construction paper to create apple prints.

- After the apple prints have dried, let kids write, "I will bear good fruit for Jesus," on their papers. Help younger kids write the words.

- Slice the unused apple halves, and give to kids for snack. As kids eat the apples, have them tell ways they'll bear good fruit by helping others.

DIRECTIONS

Before kids arrive, stick a toothpick through the ridge of a banana. Hold the banana vertically, and slide the toothpick gently back and forth in a straight line to slice the fruit inside the peel. Make sure the toothpick doesn't exit the other side. Carefully withdraw the toothpick and repeat this process at one-inch intervals. This will be the "bad" fruit.

Say: Jesus taught us that good trees produce good fruit. If we're like good trees, we'll treat others with love. But bad trees produce bad fruit. Bad fruit is being mean to others.

Sometimes fruit looks good on the outside when it's bad inside. Hand the bad banana to one child and the good one to another child. Say: Peel your fruit!

As the bad fruit is peeled, slices will fall.

Read aloud **Matthew 7:17-20.** Then say: Jesus wants us to be good trees that grow good fruit to share with others.

(Excerpted from *Show Me! Devotions* by Susan Lingo. © Group Publishing, Inc.)

LIFT YOUR HEARTS

Kids learn that Jesus carries our burdens.
Text: Matthew 11:28-30

WHAT YOU'LL NEED:

You'll need a Bible, a red permanent marker, a hard-boiled egg, ½ cup of salt, a paper cup, a spoon, a table, and a clear jar half-full of water.

ALLERGY ALERT
See page 10.

FOR EXTRA IMPACT:

- Have kids each write a worry or fear on a construction paper heart. Have kids form pairs, trade hearts, and pray for each other's concerns.

- Encourage kids to bring the hearts the following week, and let kids share any praise reports.

- Write the words to **Matthew 11:28** on a bulletin board, and let kids tape the hearts on the board.

DIRECTIONS

Before class, use a red permanent marker to draw a heart on a hard-boiled egg. Pour the salt into a paper cup with "Jesus" written on the side. Place the jar of water, a spoon, the salt, and the hard-boiled egg on a table.

Hold the hard-boiled egg so kids can see the heart. Say: Sometimes our hearts feel heavy with worries or fears. What's one fear or worry you've had?

Say: When our hearts become full of worries and fears, they sink inside us. Drop the egg into the jar of water, and say: Who can take away our worries and fears and make our hearts light? Jesus can!

Pour the salt into the jar. As you stir the water, say: Let's see what the Bible says about Jesus lifting our hearts.

Read aloud **Matthew 11:28-30** and continue stirring the water. Say: Jesus wants us to give him our worries and fears.

When the egg rises to the top and floats, say: When we give our worries and fears to Jesus, our hearts become lighter! Then ask: What's one worry or fear you can give Jesus this week?

(Excerpted from *Show Me! Devotions* by Susan Lingo. © Group Publishing, Inc.)

CHOOSE YOUR PATH

Kids learn about following Jesus.
Text: John 14:6

WHAT YOU'LL NEED:

You'll need a Bible, a clear glass full of water, a 3x5 card, pen, a book, and a table.

- Have kids write the words of **John 14:6** on one side of an index card and "I choose to follow God's path!" on the other side.

- Have kids pray silently, asking God's forgiveness for those things they've done wrong. Then have kids read aloud together the Scripture verse on their index cards.

DIRECTIONS

Before class, fill a clear glass with water. On a 3x5 card, draw a thick 3-inch-long arrow pointing to the left, and write "evil" across the bottom. Set the glass and the card on a table.

Ask: Who can tell about a time you were lost? How did you feel when you found your way back?

Pick up the card, and keep turning it around so the arrow points in different directions. Say: When we're lost, we don't know which way to go.

Then set the card back on the table with the arrow pointing to the left, and prop it up with a book. Ask: What things can turn us in the wrong direction? How can we stay on the right path to God?

Read aloud **John 14:6.** Hold up the glass and say: Following Jesus is the only way to stay on the right path to God. The Bible says that Jesus is the living water.

Set the glass of water about 5 inches in front of the arrow. The arrow on the card should now be pointing to the right, and "evil" should now read "live."

Say: Following Jesus isn't a trick—it's the truth! In fact, Jesus is the only true way to God!

(Excerpted from *Show Me! Devotions* by Susan Lingo. © Group Publishing, Inc.)

NEW TESTAMENT

CHAPTER THREE

MULTIPLE VERSES

A PURE HEART

Kids learn that God wants us to keep our hearts pure.
Text: James 5:16 and Psalm 51:10

WHAT YOU'LL NEED:

You'll need a Bible, pretzels, a pitcher of clean water, paper cups, and a clear plastic bottle, Fill the plastic bottle halfway with water, and add several spoonfuls of dirt.

ALLERGY ALERT
See page 10.

FOR EXTRA IMPACT:

- Ask: Why does God want us to keep our hearts pure? How can sin in our lives prevent us from loving and serving God the way we should?

- Give each child a large construction paper heart with "'Create in me a pure heart, O God'—Psalm 51:10" written on it. Let kids decorate their hearts with markers and stickers.

- Encourage kids to take their hearts home and hang them in their rooms. Remind kids to confess their sins and keep their hearts pure.

DIRECTIONS

Give each child a handful of pretzels. Munch a few pretzels yourself.

Say: I love pretzels, but they make me thirsty! Fortunately, I brought a bottle of refreshing water!

Hold up the bottle of dirty water. Ask: Would you like a drink? Why or why not? I'll just add some clean water.

Pour a little clean water into the dirty bottle. Ask: There, did that help?

Say: Our hearts can be like this water bottle. When we sin or do bad things, our hearts get dirty. What can you do when your heart gets dirty with sin?

Read aloud **James 5:16** and **Psalm 51:10.** Say: It's important to tell our sins to God and let him clean our hearts.

Pray: God, help us confess our sins to you. Give us pure hearts to love and serve you. In Jesus' name, amen.

Pour each child a cup of clean water.

MULTIPLE VERSES

BUBBLE GUM HEARTS

Kids learn about humility.
Text: 1 Peter 5:5-6; Proverbs 21:4

WHAT YOU'LL NEED:

You'll need a Bible and a gumball for each child.

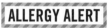
ALLERGY ALERT
See page 10.

FOR EXTRA IMPACT:

- Read aloud **Proverbs 21:4.** Ask: Why do you think having haughty eyes and a proud heart is a sin?

- Ask: Why does God want us to do what is right and just?

- Ask: What are things we can do to keep our hearts humble?

DIRECTIONS

Give each child a gumball. Have kids turn to a partner and describe their gumball.

Say: Our gumballs are like our hearts when we're overly proud. I'm not just talking about feeling good about ourselves; I'm talking about puffing ourselves up and thinking we're better than others. What are some things people do when they're overly proud?

Read aloud **1 Peter 5:5-6.** Say: Pop your gum into your mouth. As you chew, what's happening to your gum? When we humble ourselves, we tell God that we're sorry that we've been overly proud. We say that we know that God is so much greater than us. What happens to our hearts when we humble ourselves before God?

Say: Blow a big bubble with your gum. Being humble—or not overly proud—makes our hearts bubble over with joy.

MULTIPLE VERSES

BUILDING KINDNESS

Kids learn about kindness.
Text: Ephesians 4:29; 1 Thessalonians 5:11

WHAT YOU'LL NEED:

You'll need a Bible and 8 wooden blocks for each pair.

FOR EXTRA IMPACT:

- Read aloud **1 Thessalonians 5:11.** Ask: Why should we encourage one another?

- Ask: What happens when we build each other up? What happens when we don't?

- Have kids turn to their partners and say a few encouraging phrases.

MULTIPLE VERSES

DIRECTIONS

Form pairs, and give each pair eight blocks. Say: With your partner, use five blocks to make a block building. Spread out at least an arm's length from other pairs.

Allow kids time to build their structures. Then say: Now stand by your building and use your three extra blocks to knock down other buildings. You can protect your building, but you only have 10 seconds. Go!

After 10 seconds, ask: How did it feel to have others tear down your buildings? How does it feel when people tear you down with their words?

Read aloud **Ephesians 4:29.** Say: When people are unkind to us, they tear down our feelings just as we tore down the buildings. When we're unkind to others, we tear down their feelings. But God has called us to build up others.

Ask: What are some things you can say to build up people and help them feel good?

For each answer, have the children pick up a block and add it to another pair's building. Lead the group in a prayer asking God to help them love and build up others.

CHANGED!

Kids learn about the gospel.
Text: 1 Corinthians 15:3-4;
2 Corinthians 5:17

WHAT YOU'LL NEED:

You'll need a Bible, bowls, spoons, vinegar, egg dye, and a hard-boiled egg for each child.

ALLERGY ALERT
See page 10.

FOR EXTRA IMPACT:

- Ask: What do you think it means that we are new creations in Christ?

- Ask: How are we changed when we follow Jesus?

- Have kids form pairs and pray together, asking God to guide them as they share their faith in Jesus with others.

DIRECTIONS

Read aloud **1 Corinthians 15:3-4.** Say: These verses contain the gospel that we celebrate at Easter. Let's read them again and pick out the parts of the gospel story.

Read the Scripture again. Help kids understand that the heart of the gospel is Christ's death, burial, and resurrection for the forgiveness of our sins.

Say: I have some egghead friends who need to hear the gospel.

Give each child an egg. Have children each tell the gospel to their egg. Say: When we tell others the gospel and they follow Jesus, something wonderful happens.

Have kids dip their eggs in the bowls of dye. Read aloud **2 Corinthians 5:17.** Say: People who believe in Jesus are changed. Give your egg to a friend who doesn't yet believe in Jesus. Tell your friend about the gospel you believe.

COLD HEARTS

Kids learn about the effects of sin.
Text: Matthew 24:12; Proverbs 28:14;
Proverbs 4:23

WHAT YOU'LL NEED:

You'll need a Bible, paper towels, an empty soft-drink bottle, a hole punch, yarn, an ice-cube tray, water, and a freezer.

FOR EXTRA IMPACT:

- Read aloud **Proverbs 28:14.** Ask: How does hardening our hearts lead to trouble?

- Read aloud **Proverbs 4:23.** Ask: What are things we can do to guard our hearts from sin?

- Give children heart stickers to remind them to guard their hearts against sin.

DIRECTIONS

Before kids arrive, cut out a 1-inch heart from an empty soft-drink bottle. Punch a hole in the heart, and thread a 6-inch length of yarn through it. Suspend the heart in an ice cube tray, ensuring that the loose ends of the yarn stay out of the tray. Add water and freeze.

Gather the kids together, and read aloud **Matthew 24:12.** Then show kids the ice-encased heart.

Say: Sin makes hearts cold; and people with cold hearts don't treat each other well. We sure can see sin everywhere. What could melt this heart?

Give each child a paper towel. Have children work together to melt the ice and free the heart.

Ask: How easy or difficult was it to free the cold heart? What needs to happen to melt people's cold hearts? How would the world be different if no hearts were cold?

Say: Only Jesus can thaw our hearts. As we let Christ's love fill our hearts, we'll be an example that affects coldhearted people around us.

MULTIPLE VERSES

FREE AT LAST

Kids learn about the freedom to worship God.
Text: Acts 5:25-29; Deuteronomy 28:2

WHAT YOU'LL NEED:

You'll need a Bible. For each pair of kids, you'll need four 10-inch strips of fabric and a paper with the following instructions written on it: (1) Don't use the word "I" (eyes); (2) Don't talk with your hands (hands); (3) Don't move your feet (feet); (4) Don't use the word "God" (mouth).

FOR EXTRA IMPACT:

- Ask: Why is it more important to obey God than men?

- Read aloud **Deuteronomy 28:2.** Ask: Why do you think God blesses us when we obey him?

- Ask: What are things we can do that will help us obey God?

▶ DIRECTIONS

Say: Find a partner. Choose which partner will be the Talker and which will be the Listener. I'm going to give the Listeners some rules and fabric strips. Don't let your Talker see the rules.

Say: You Listeners need to make sure the Talkers don't break any of the rules as they talk. If your Talker breaks one of the rules, use the fabric to bind up the area that's listed on the rules. Talkers, you have three minutes to talk. Go!

Allow three minutes. Ask: How did you feel during this activity? How did it feel to have your freedoms taken away? How would it feel to have your freedom to worship or talk about God taken away?

Read aloud **Acts 5:25-29.** Say: Peter said we must obey God instead of men. Peter meant that it's more important to honor God than to be afraid of the rules people have made to keep us from talking about our faith.

LEFTOVER HURT

Kids learn about anger.
Text: Ephesians 4:26; Psalm 4:4

WHAT YOU'LL NEED:

You'll need a Bible and 1 inflated, tied-off balloon for each child.

FOR EXTRA IMPACT:

- Read aloud **Psalm 4:4.** Ask: How is this verse like or unlike **Ephesians 4:26?**

- Ask: Why do you think God tells us in both the Old and New Testaments not to go to bed angry?

- Ask: Why does the Bible tell us to search our hearts and be silent? What happens when we're silent before God?

DIRECTIONS

Say: Raise your hand if you've ever been angry. Can you show me your angry face? I'm going to give you each a balloon that you can sit on and pop. Try to make an angry face while you pop your balloon.

Have kids sit on their balloons, then ask: How did you feel when you popped your balloon? What's left of your balloon?

Read aloud **Ephesians 4:26.** Then say: If we go to bed mad enough to pop, there's usually something leftover in the morning from our anger. We may still be angry at our friends, or we may still feel yucky in the morning. God doesn't want us to go to bed angry. God wants us to ask for forgiveness from any person we've hurt. And God also wants us to forgive anyone who's made us mad enough to pop. That'll make us feel better, too!

Say: Let's pray. God, help us forgive friends who hurt us, and help us to ask our friends to forgive us. In Jesus' name, amen.

MULTIPLE VERSES

LET THERE BE LIGHT

Kids celebrate Christmas with this living Nativity.
Text: Isaiah 60:1; John 8:12; Matthew 5:14, 16; Genesis 1:3

WHAT YOU'LL NEED:

You'll need to list the following on a chalkboard or newsprint: baby Jesus, Mary, Joseph, shepherd, wise man, roof, star, angel, manger, gift, and swaddling clothes.

FOR EXTRA IMPACT:

- Ask: What does it mean to you that Jesus is the light of the world?

- Ask: How can we be lights to the world? How does that glorify God?

- Have kids think of actions they can do this week to share God's love with others.

DIRECTIONS

Say: We're going to experience a little bit of Christmas today.

Turn down the lights. Choose one person to be baby Jesus and tell why. For example, "Your love for people reminds me of Jesus." Give that person a lighted candle, and place that person in the living Nativity scene. Then have that person choose someone who represents another part of the Nativity, tell why, place that person in the living Nativity, and light his or her candle.

After everyone is placed, read aloud these Scriptures:

"Arise, shine; for your light has come, and the glory of the Lord rises upon you" **(Isaiah 60:1).**

"I am the light of the world. Whoever follows me will never walk in darkness, but will have the light of life" **(John 8:12).**

"You are the light of the world…Let your light shine before men, that they may see your good deeds and praise your Father in heaven" **(Matthew 5:14, 16).**

"And God said, 'Let there be light,' and there was light" **(Genesis 1:3).**

Pray: Dear God, thank you for sending Jesus, the light, into a dark world. Help us be your light and reveal Jesus during this Christmas season.

MULTIPLE VERSES

LIGHT OF THE WORLD

Kids learn about the light of Jesus.
Text: Luke 2:1-20; John 1:9-12

WHAT YOU'LL NEED:

You'll need a Bible, a trick candle that lights again after being blown out, a drip tray to go around the candle, matches, a Christmas CD or cassette, and a CD or cassette player.

FOR EXTRA IMPACT:

- Ask: What does it mean to be a child of God?

- Ask: As a child of God, what can you do to show the light of Jesus to others?

- Give each child a mini-flashlight to keep as a reminder to share the light of Jesus to others.

DIRECTIONS

Dim the lights if possible, and softly play Christmas music. While the music plays, light the trick candle and describe the birth of Jesus, the light of the world, from **Luke 2:1-20.** You must talk for at least 30 seconds for the trick candle to work.

Say: Turn to a partner and name one person who tried to kill Jesus.

Pause and let kids answer. If kids have trouble thinking of people, mention Herod, Satan, the Pharisees, and Judas. Say: Now let's try to blow out the light.

When you blow out the candle, it'll relight. Say: Many people tried to "blow out" the Light of the World, but what happened? On Easter, Jesus rose from the dead! They couldn't blow out Jesus' light.

Read **John 1:9-12.** Ask: Who or what do you think is trying to blow out the Light of the World today? Why should we help others know that Jesus is the light of the world? Explain.

MULTIPLE VERSES

LOVE IN ANY LANGUAGE

Kids learn about Pentecost.
Text: Acts 2:1-12; Psalm 75:1

WHAT YOU'LL NEED:

You'll need a Bible and a teenager to play the role of a foreigner who can't speak English.

FOR EXTRA IMPACT:

- Teach kids the Hebrew word for wonderful: *Pala'* pronounced "paw-law."

- Read aloud **Psalm 75:1.** Then have kids tell wonderful things God has done in their lives.

- Write the following words and caption on a bulletin board: *"Maravilloso, merveilleux, meragivlioso, wunderbar, Pala'*—God is WONDERFUL in any language!"* Let kids decorate the bulletin board with ribbons, stickers, and other craft supplies.

▶ DIRECTIONS

Introduce the "foreigner" to the group. Say: This person doesn't speak our language but needs to know about God's love. How can you tell someone something about God's love if that person doesn't speak English?

Say: Find a partner and choose one way to tell your message without speaking English.

After a minute, let kids present their ideas to the foreigner. They might pantomime or do something kind for the person.

Ask: Do you think our friend got the message? When the first Christians were spreading the gospel, people from all countries needed to hear it.

Read aloud **Acts 2:1-12.** Say: With God's help, many different people understood his message of love. We need God's help to share the message, too. Let's pray. God, help us tell others how much you love them. Amen.

MULTIPLE VERSES

MARY'S DILEMMA

Kids learn about the Resurrection.
Text: Mark 16:1-7; 2 Corinthians 2:14-15

WHAT YOU'LL NEED:

You'll need a Bible and a cup of shortening mixed with several drops of potpourri refresher oil. You'll also need 4x4 squares of wax paper, a plastic knife, black construction paper for each child, and an iron (with adult supervision).

FOR EXTRA IMPACT:

- Encourage kids to place their papers by their beds at home. As kids awake each morning, they should let the sweet fragrance remind them to offer God thanks for his sweet gift of Jesus.

- Read aloud **2 Corinthians 2:14-15.** Ask: How is knowing Jesus like a sweet fragrance?

- Ask: What does the Bible mean when it says that we are the aroma of Christ to God? How can we be the aroma of Jesus to others?

DIRECTIONS

Read aloud **Mark 16:1-7.** Say: This ointment may be a little like what the women were taking to Jesus' tomb on the first Easter morning.

Give each child a blob of ointment on a square of wax paper. Have children make ointment designs on their black paper that remind them of Easter. Fold the papers in half with the ointment inside, and iron them. The designs will come through the back of the paper.

Say: Just as the paper couldn't keep the ointment in, the grave couldn't keep Jesus in. We can rejoice because Jesus is risen!

Close in prayer.

MULTIPLE VERSES

MUFFLED

Kids learn about faith sharing.
Text: John 3:16; Philemon 1:6

WHAT YOU'LL NEED:

You'll need Bibles, large marshmallows, cups, and water.

ALLERGY ALERT
See page 10

FOR EXTRA IMPACT:

- Ask: What are three ways you can share your faith with others?

- Have kids turn to partners and tell specific things they can say when sharing their faith with others. Let kids practice with their partners.

- Have kids each think of one person they can share their faith with during the coming week. Have kids report back the following week.

▶ DIRECTIONS

Give each child a Bible and six large marshmallows. Have kids stuff the marshmallows in their mouths, then together read aloud **John 3:16.** After kids swallow or spit out their marshmallows, offer them a drink of water.

Ask: Was it easy or difficult to talk with marshmallows in your mouth? Explain. How important was the message in the verse you read? How important is it for us to share the gospel with people? Our speech was muffled by the marshmallows. What things can muffle our ability to share the gospel? Who do you know who needs to hear the gospel?

Read aloud **Philemon 1:6.** Say: I pray that each of you will be active in sharing your faith, so that you will have a full understanding of every good thing you have in Christ.

MULTIPLE VERSES

NO HIDING PLACE

Kids learn we can't hide from God.
Text: Genesis 3:1-13; Psalm 66:20

WHAT YOU'LL NEED:

You'll need a Bible and a cover such as a large tarp, a sheet, or a parachute.

FOR EXTRA IMPACT:

- Ask: How do you think God feels when we talk to him in prayer? When we don't?
- Read aloud **Psalm 66:20.** Ask: Why would God never withhold his love from us?
- Ask: How does knowing that nothing can separate us from the love of God affect your life?

MULTIPLE VERSES

DIRECTIONS

Say: Let's see if we can hide from God. I've brought something I think might help us do that.

Get beneath the cover with the kids. Then ask: Have we hidden from God? Can God see us under here? Why or why not?

Say: We can't hide from God; he can see us anywhere we go or anywhere we hide.

Remove the cover, and read aloud **Genesis 3:1-13.** Say: When Adam and Eve disobeyed God, they tried to hide themselves from God. Have you ever done anything bad and then tried to hide? Do you think God wants us to hide from him when we do something wrong? What does God want us to do when we do something wrong?

Say: God knows when we do something wrong, but he wants us to talk to him about it and not hide. God doesn't want to punish us. God wants to forgive us and help us change. When we talk to God in prayer and don't hide, God can help us grow to be stronger Christians.

Say: Let's pray. Thank you, God, for knowing everything about us. Help us tell you when we do something wrong. Help us ask for forgiveness. Thank you for loving us! In Jesus' name, amen.

PACK IT IN

Kids learn that Jesus is with them at school.
Text: Jeremiah 33:3; Galatians 5:22-23

WHAT YOU'LL NEED:

You'll need a Bible and a child's backpack containing these items: a banana with the fruit of the Spirit from **Galatians 5:22-23** written on it with a permanent marker, a hand weight, a cell phone, a gold-paper heart, a box of Band-Aids, and funny glasses.

FOR EXTRA IMPACT:

- Have kids write, "'Call to me and I will answer you'— Jeremiah 33:3" on an index card. Help younger kids.

- Give each child a gold heart sticker and a Band-Aid. Have kids write "Jesus" on their heart stickers and on their bandages and then stick them on the index card.

- Encourage kids to carry the cards in their backpacks as reminders that Jesus is with them at school.

DIRECTIONS

Say: School is starting soon. I hope you haven't forgotten to pack. Just in case, I packed these things for you.

Pull out the banana, and say: You'll need the fruit of love, joy, peace, patience, goodness, gentleness, kindness, faithfulness, and self-control.

Pull out the hand weight, and say: Exercising your trust in God will make your faith muscles stronger.

Pull out the cell phone. Read aloud **Jeremiah 33:3.** Say: Don't forget to call on God with prayer.

Pull out the gold heart, and say: You'll be tempted to sin, but keep your heart pure.

Pull out the Band-Aids, and say: School can be tough. But be like Jesus and be kind to everyone.

Pull out the funny glasses, and say: You need God's eyes to know the things that are true and the things that aren't true. If you have all these things in your backpack, I know you'll have a great new school year.

Close with a prayer of blessing for the children in the new school year.

MULTIPLE VERSES

PURE MILK

Kids learn about spiritual growth.
Text: 1 Peter 2:2; Matthew 26:41

WHAT YOU'LL NEED:

You'll need a Bible, 1 cup of warm milk, a clear plastic 12-ounce glass, a tablespoon, a spoon, and vinegar.

FOR EXTRA IMPACT:

- Have kids form two groups. Have one group list unhealthy temptations and the other group list spiritually healthy things we can do.

- Have groups read aloud their lists to the class. Then read aloud **Matthew 26:41.**

- Ask: What does "the spirit is willing but the body is weak" mean? How does feeding our bodies spiritually healthy things make us stronger?

MULTIPLE VERSES

DIRECTIONS

Say: When we become Christians, we need to feed our spirits good things to help us grow spiritually, just as we feed our bodies healthy things to help us grow physically. Let's say that this milk represents healthy spiritual food. What is healthy spiritual food?

Pour half of the milk into the glass. Say: Wow! That's a lot of spiritual nutrition. Once in a while, we might be tempted to put in some bad stuff, like watching a movie we know doesn't please or honor God.

Stir in a tablespoon of vinegar. Say: But then we go right back to putting in healthy things such as reading our Bibles or praying.

Pour in more milk. Say: Another temptation comes along, and we give into it.

Stir in two tablespoons of vinegar. Ask: Who wants to drink this milk now? How is this mixture like or unlike mixing good and bad spiritual food in our lives?

Read aloud **1 Peter 2:2.** Say: God wants us to keep our lives pure. That requires feeding ourselves a steady diet of healthy spiritual food.

ROCK-SOLID SIN

Kids learn about the burden of sin.
Text: Hebrews 12:1-2; Psalm 32:5

WHAT YOU'LL NEED:

You'll need a Bible, rocks of various sizes (enough for each child to have 2), and a basket.

FOR EXTRA IMPACT:

- Read aloud **Psalm 32:5.** Ask: What happens in our lives when we ask for and accept God's forgiveness?

- Ask: How would you feel if you weren't sure that God would forgive you when you asked? How can you thank God for forgiving you?

- Have kids tell things they can do to guard themselves against sin.

DIRECTIONS

Have each child select two rocks. Tell children to keep one rock in each hand at all times throughout your time together. Continue with a regularly planned class during which the children keep the rocks in their hands, no matter what the activity. Some children will complain that their rocks are heavy, some will play with them, some will have difficulty doing the activities. Encourage them not to set down the rocks.

Near the end of class, lead children in this discussion. Ask: How easy or difficult was it to hold onto these rocks? How is carrying around sin like or unlike carrying around these rocks?

Read aloud **Hebrews 12:1-2.** Say: Think of a personal sin you need to confess to God. Put aside your rocks in this basket as you silently confess your sin to God.

Close by thanking God for forgiveness of sins.

MULTIPLE VERSES

SOAKING UP THE SPIRIT

Kids learn about being filled with the Holy Spirit.
Text: Ephesians 5:18; Psalm 51:11

WHAT YOU'LL NEED:

You'll need a Bible; a hard, dry sponge; and a bucket of water.

FOR EXTRA IMPACT:

- Give each child a piece of dry sponge. Have kids dip their sponges in a bucket of water as they say, "God, help me to soak up your Holy Spirit."

- Read aloud **Psalm 51:11.** Then pray to thank God for his gift of the Holy Spirit.

- Have kids wring out their sponges and take them home. Suggest that when they're feeling "dry," they can soak their sponges in water and remember to ask God to fill them with his Holy Spirit.

MULTIPLE VERSES

DIRECTIONS

Say: Take a look at this hard, dry sponge.

Let the children feel the sponge. Ask: What can you use this dry sponge for? When a sponge is dry, it's pretty useless. What needs to happen for this sponge to become useful?

Submerge the sponge in water, and wring it out. Ask: What can you do with it now? What made the difference?

Read aloud **Ephesians 5:18.** Ask: What does this verse say? How are we like the sponge and the water?

Say: Before we know God we're "dry" and useless spiritually. When we give our lives to the Lord and let him fill us with his Spirit, we become ready to do the tasks God has for us. How can we soak up the Holy Spirit and get ready for what God wants us to do?

SPIRITUAL WARDROBE

Kids learn about new life in Christ.
Ephesians 4:20-29; Philippians 4:8

WHAT YOU'LL NEED:

You'll need a Bible, newsprint, tape, and markers.

FOR EXTRA IMPACT:

- Ask: How can we protect and guard our minds?

- Read aloud **Philippians 4:8.** Ask: Why should we think about praiseworthy things?

- Ask: How do you think your life might change if you think about things that are right, pure, and lovely?

DIRECTIONS

Use newsprint and tape to make paper clothing on a child. Have the child with the paper clothing stand with you.

Say: Let's look at things we do that God says he's not happy about. For example, God doesn't like lying. Let's write lying on this costume. Each time you think of something, call it out, and I'll write it on the costume.

Read aloud everything listed on the costume. Then read **Ephesians 4:20-29.**

Say: The Bible says to take off the old self and put on the new self. Let's help [child's name] take off this costume of the old self.

Have children rip off the paper clothing. Then ask: What does God mean when he tells us to "put on the new self"? How can we do that? What are some things that would be on our new self's costume?

Say: The new self is the exact opposite of the old self. For example, instead of stealing, we work hard. Let's ask God to help us put on the new self.

Close in prayer.

MULTIPLE VERSES

STORM BREAK

Kids learn about trusting Jesus.
Text: Mark 4:35-41; Psalm 28:7

WHAT YOU'LL NEED:

Nothing! This is a prop-free, prep-free devotion.

FOR EXTRA IMPACT:

- Read aloud **Psalm 28:7.** Ask: How are we helped when we trust in the Lord?

- Say: Just as Jesus calmed the storm, we can trust the Lord to be our strength and our shield. When do you feel like you need God's protection?

- Ask: Why are we to give thanks to the Lord in song? Turn on praise music and let kids praise God together.

MULTIPLE VERSES

▶ DIRECTIONS

Say: I'll read a story from the Bible in **Mark 4:35-41.** Follow my actions.

The disciples stood by the Sea of Galilee. *(Stand with hands on hips.)*

Jesus said, "Let's go to the other side." *(Wave to tell everyone to come along.)*

So they got in the boat, and they rowed out to sea. *(Make rowing motions.)*

Jesus fell asleep. *(Lay head on hands.)*

Wind blew against the boat. *(Wave arms to imitate big gusts of wind.)*

Water washed into the boat. They tried to bail it out. *(Pretend to bail.)*

"Somebody wake Jesus!" they yelled. *(Pretend to shake Jesus.)*

Jesus awoke and said, "Hush, be still." *(Hold out hand against the wind.)*

And the wind died down. *(Let your arms wave and then drop.)*

They continued to row to the other side. *(Pretend to row.)* But they were never the same after that.

Turn to a partner, and answer these questions: Is there a stormy area in your life? How can you trust Jesus to calm that storm?

SWEET LOVE

Kids learn about God's love and discipline.
Text: Proverbs 3:11-12; Psalm 94:12

WHAT YOU'LL NEED:

You'll need a Bible, WarHead candies, and a large, clear plastic heart.

See page 10.

FOR EXTRA IMPACT:

- Ask: How do you usually respond to discipline? How do you think we should respond? Explain.

- Read aloud **Psalm 94:12.** Ask: Why is it a blessing to be disciplined?

- Ask: Do you think God would discipline us if he didn't love us? Explain.

DIRECTIONS

Before kids arrive, remove the wrappers from WarHead candies, one per child, and put them in a large, clear plastic heart.

Show kids the heart. Ask: What does this heart remind you of? What are some sweet ways your parents love you?

Say: Let's have a piece of candy to remind us of our parents' love.

Have each child take one piece of candy and eat it. Ask: What's wrong?

Encourage children to keep sucking on the candy because it'll become sweet. Say: Sometimes when our parents discipline us, it's not sweet; it's sour like the candy.

Read aloud **Proverbs 3:11-12.** Ask: Why do parents discipline their children? Why does God discipline us?

Ask: How does your candy taste now? God's love for us is sweet like the candy is now. Even though it may seem sour when God disciplines us, it's because of his sweet love that he corrects us.

Close in prayer.

MULTIPLE VERSES

THE RIGHT PATH

Kids learn about following God's direction.
Text: Psalm 119:105; Romans 15:4

WHAT YOU'LL NEED:

You'll need a Bible, a homemade map, and a road map.

FOR EXTRA IMPACT:

- Instead of hiding one Bible, let kids form groups, and give each group a map to a hidden Bible.

- Have groups read aloud **Romans 15:4.** Read or paraphrase the passage for younger kids.

- Ask: How does the Bible bring us hope?

MULTIPLE VERSES

▶ DIRECTIONS

Before kids arrive, hide a Bible in the room. Make an easy map with cut-out pictures and simple words so children can find the Bible in about two minutes. You'll also need a road map.

Hold up a road map. Ask: How does this map help people?

Give kids the map you made, and have them find the Bible. Say: Use this map to find something special hidden in this room.

Say: You found the map God has given us for our lives—the Bible.

Read aloud **Psalm 119:105.** Say: God's Word shows us what we need to do to follow him on the right path.

Say: I'll read some directions. If you think they're from the Bible, raise your hand:

Only fight if you think it's right.

Love your enemies, do good to those who hate you.

A gossip betrays a confidence; so avoid a man who talks too much.

Don't tell a lie unless you absolutely have to.

Direct me in the path of your commands, for there I find delight.

Say: Let's pray and ask God to help us do the right things to stay on his path.

TOWER OF CONFUSION

Kids learn about the Tower of Babel.
Text: Genesis 11:1-9; Ephesians 4:29

WHAT YOU'LL NEED:

You'll need a Bible. For each group, you'll need 10 paper-towel rolls cut in thirds, transparent tape, and 5 slips of paper with one of the following directions written on each slip: "Say the opposite of what you mean," "Remain silent and use no body language," "Gesture with your hands," "Ask questions," and "Talk in baby talk."

FOR EXTRA IMPACT:

- Read aloud **Ephesians 4:29.** Ask: What are things you can say to your family members to build them up?

- Ask: How do words of encouragement benefit those who listen?

- Ask: How does your attitude change when people offer you words of encouragement?

 DIRECTIONS

Form groups of five. Give each group its supplies. Tell kids to take one paper slip and keep their instructions secret. Say: Build a tower as high as you can in three minutes. Work together, but communicate only the way your paper instructs.

After the allotted time, ask: How did it feel to communicate with one another? Explain. Have you ever felt the same way when you're trying to talk to your family? Why or why not?

Read aloud **Genesis 11:1-9.** Ask: Why do you think God confused the languages of the people?

God doesn't want us to rebel like the people in our story, but he wants us to communicate with our family members and work together.

TRASH YOUR SINS

Kids learn about getting rid of our sins.
Text: Romans 5:6-11; Psalm 51:1-2

WHAT YOU'LL NEED:

You'll need a Bible, newspapers, markers, a large garbage bag, and a pack of baby wipes.

FOR EXTRA IMPACT:

- Some newspaper has more ink residue than others. If your paper has less residue, have kids play with the wads to get more ink on their hands before tossing them into the garbage bag.

- Read aloud **Psalm 51:1-2.** Ask: How was using the baby wipes to clean our hands, like or unlike how God cleanses us from our sins?

- Ask: Why does God have compassion on us? What does that tell you about God?

DIRECTIONS

Give each child a marker and several sheets of newspaper. Place a garbage bag in the center of the room.

Say: The Bible says that everybody sins. Write the name of one sin on each sheet of newspaper, then wad it up and pitch it in this garbage bag. Write as many sins as you can think of.

After three minutes, have kids gather around the bag of sins. Say: When we mess with sin, we get dirty.

Read aloud **Romans 5:6-8.** Then hand each child a baby wipe.

Ask: How does it feel to have dirty hands? How does it feel when you sin? How can we be clean?

Read **Romans 5:8-11.** Ask: What has God done for us to make us clean? Why do you think God did this for you?

Close in prayer, thanking God for sending Jesus to die for us.

MULTIPLE VERSES

UNSEEN PRESENCE

Kids learn about faith.
Text: Hebrews 11:1; 2 Corinthians 5:7

WHAT YOU'LL NEED:

You'll need a blindfold, a large bowl filled with uncooked white rice, and 25 small paper clips for each group of four. You'll also need a Bible.

FOR EXTRA IMPACT:

- Let other kids in the group have a turn trying to find the paper clips.

- Read **2 Corinthians 5:7.** Ask: How is this verse like or unlike **Hebrews 11:1?** Why does God want us to live by faith and not by sight?

- Lead kids in asking God to strengthen their faith in him every day.

DIRECTIONS

Give each group its blindfold, bowl of rice, and paper clips. Say: In your group, choose one person to be your Seeker. Blindfold your Seeker.

Say: Now, Seekers, you have one minute to find as many paper clips as you can in the bowl of rice. Ready? Go!

Call time after one minute. Say: Take off your blindfold. How many paper clips did you find? How easy or difficult was it to find the paper clips in the rice? What made it easy? What made it difficult?

Read aloud **Hebrews 11:1.** Just as our friends hunted for something they couldn't see or feel, God asks us to believe in things we can't see or feel. Have you ever had to believe something that you couldn't see or feel? Explain. How can you be sure that you're believing in something real if you can't see or feel it?

Say: The paper clips were here all the time; and God is here all the time too. We can believe God even though we don't always see or feel what we're believing in.

WE ARE ONE

Kids learn about Christlikeness.
Text: 1 Corinthians 6:17; Matthew 5:16

WHAT YOU'LL NEED:

You'll need a Bible, and 1 teaspoon of each of the following in a separate baby food jar: powdered milk, baking soda, oil, and plain water. You'll also need a bottle of white vinegar.

FOR EXTRA IMPACT:

- Ask: Does your behavior show that you believe in Jesus? How can you do better?

- Read aloud **Matthew 5:16.** Ask: How can we let our light shine before others?

- Why is it important that we be a light to others? What can you do today to show that you love Jesus?

MULTIPLE VERSES

DIRECTIONS

Say: Jesus showed his followers how to truly "walk the talk" of Christianity by joining together with him! This vinegar will represent Jesus' teachings.

Add a little vinegar to each substance, and explain the reactions in order. Say: Some people curdle like this powdered milk. They complain about how hard it is to follow God and they never grow. Some Christians have lots of fizz (baking soda) when they first hear Jesus' words, but very little follow-through. Some people never learn how to mix (oil) Jesus' words into their lives.

Ask: But what do you notice about the vinegar mixed with this pure water? Does it look like water or vinegar? (Let the kids smell the solution.) Does it smell like water or vinegar?

Read aloud **1 Corinthians 6:17.** Say: The water has become part of the vinegar. In the same way, we need to be Christians who become so much like Jesus that people see him when they look at us.

WORTHWHILE FAITH

Kids learn about the value of faith.
Text: 1 Corinthians 15:12-20; Mark 11:22

WHAT YOU'LL NEED:

You'll need a Bible, a yo-yo without a string, a camera without film, empty candy wrappers, and a piece of candy for each child.

ALLERGY ALERT
See page 10.

FOR EXTRA IMPACT:

- Ask: How is the sweetness of the candy like or unlike the sweetness of our faith?

- Read aloud **Mark 11:22.** Ask: What does it mean to have faith in God? How will you show this week that you have faith in God?

- Ask: How has God proven himself worthy of our faith and trust in him? How can you thank God for his faithfulness?

DIRECTIONS

Ask: Would anyone like to play with my yo-yo?

Give the yo-yo without a string. Say: Hmmm, sorry. I guess you can't use a yo-yo without a string. Even though that didn't work, I'd like to take a picture of all of you. Smile! Oops. It seems that my camera doesn't have any film. Well, maybe a piece of candy will cheer us up.

Pass out empty candy wrappers. Say: Oh, no! There's no candy in these wrappers.

Ask: What was wrong with these things? The yo-yo, camera, and candy wrappers are worthless without the string, film, and candy. What does it mean when something is worthless?

Read aloud **1 Corinthians 15:12-20** in an easy-to-understand translation. Say: The Bible tells us that if Jesus didn't come back to life, then our faith is as worthless as a yo-yo without a string, as useless as a camera without film, and as disappointing as a candy wrapper with no candy.

Say: But Jesus did rise from the dead! Our faith is sweet because it's not worthless.

Give each child a piece of candy.

MULTIPLE VERSES

OLD TESTAMENT TEXT

NEW TESTAMENT TEXT

INDEX

INDEX

MULTIPLE SCRIPTURE TEXT

AGE-LEVEL

INDEX

THE BEST OF CHILDREN'S MINISTRY MAGAZINE: **DEVOTIONS**

INDEX

INDEX

THE BEST OF CHILDREN'S MINISTRY MAGAZINE: **DEVOTIONS**